# THE
# EASTER
# Impact

# THE EASTER
## *Impact*

### HOW THE RESURRECTION
### RESTORES AND STRENGTHENS
### OUR FAITH

GEORGES CHEVROT

Scepter

*The Easter Impact* is a revised edition of *On the Third Day*,
Scepter Dublin, 1961.
Original title in French: *The Victoire de Pâques*,
Maison de la Bonne Press, Paris, 1951.

Original *nihil obstat*: Mons. T. F. O'Reilly, vicar general.
Original *imprimatur*: Joannes Carolus, Dublin, February 27, 1961.

This revised edition © 2021 by Scepter Publishers, Inc.
First printing, 2021
Published with permission from Jean Chevrot, Paris, France.

info@scepterpublishers.org
www.scepterpublishers.org
New York
All rights reserved

Cover design: Studio Red Design
Cover art: Giovanni Antonio Galli (Lo Spadarino),
Christ displaying his wounds, 1625-1635, Oil on canvas.

Printed in the United States of America

Library of Congress Control Number: 2021945166
ISBN: 978-1-59417-433-9 (pbk)
ISBN: 978-1-59417-432-2 (eBook)

# INTRODUCTION

A nother book about the importance of Easter? Monsignor Georges Chevrot (1879–1958) tells in dramatic detail the reasons why it is so important. Easter is more than a joyous commemoration of the Lord's resurrection. It encompasses all the basic teachings of Christianity that unrolled into history with the heavy stone before the Lord's tomb in the dark of an early morning in Jerusalem over two thousand years ago. These included the untold joy of everlasting unity with God, or the unspeakable horror of eternal separation. The forgiveness of sin, the preaching of Christ's coming, and the beginning of the perhaps hundreds or thousands of centuries of efforts to bring all human beings to salvation before the world comes to an end in the Creator's good time. Everything that the Lord commanded the apostles also obliges us.

This book first appeared in French in 1951, as France and the rest of Europe were rebuilding from the destruction of World War II. Monsignor Chevrot was a seventy-two-year-old parish priest who was trying to rebuild the spiritual life of his parishioners in Paris, where he lived for all his seventy-nine years. He endured the bloodbath of World War I, and with a twenty-year interval, the four years of occupation in World War II. It is noteworthy that he never touches on these difficult years in France. It is a sign of his extraordinary supernatural spirit and a faith which embraced all souls. It is also testimony *how can everyone be expected to be supernatural?*

that the struggle to seek holiness applies to all, at all times, irrespective of the conditions in which it is sought.

Strengthening faith, <u>living supernatural virtue</u>, prayer, the Eucharist, and acts of charity all come out in a positive but demanding flow of ideas through Chevrot's writings. Part One details the doctrinal aspects of Easter starting with the key elements of its importance, then the motivations and actions of the apostles as well as the holy women and the Blessed Mother, the only one who never lost faith in her son's prediction of his resurrection. In part one's twelve short chapters, Chevrot highlights the lessons of Easter in a way that points out for each reader a path to improvement and conversion in everyday life. Part two examines in each chapter some specific lessons of Sundays and feast days, which provide something to pray about and meditate on during the Easter season.

*nature of humans is to sin*
*need to be "supernatural" to be virtuous*

# Part One
# GLORY AFTER THE CROSS

# VICTORY OVER DEATH

*For he is the true Lamb who has taken away the sins of the world; by dying he has destroyed our death, and by rising, restored our life.*

—Preface no. 1 for Easter

Easter, feast of feasts and queen of festivals, is a time for supreme rejoicing, and the Church wants our joy to be heard. "Let us rejoice," she says, "and abandon ourselves to exultations." Our Eastern co-religionists greet one another on this day with the actual words of the liturgy: "Christ is risen! He is risen indeed." With hearts raised to heaven, we give thanks to the Lord our God with unrestrained fervor, "on this day when Christ our Pasch is sacrificed." The word *Pascha* means "passage," the passing of God through our midst and our journey to God. The resurrection of Jesus is the culminating point in God's eternal plan for redeeming us. One of the first stages in this plan was the deliverance of the people of Israel from Egyptian domination. Each year the Chosen People used to commemorate the passage of the Lord who, in order to help the captives escape, smote the firstborn of Egyptian families and protected the Israelites' houses, distinguished by the lamb's blood smeared on their doors. When Pharaoh reluctantly let the Jews go, his armies tried in vain to overtake them after they crossed the Red Sea, but the Egyptian pursuers were swallowed up by the waters which rolled back over them so that the children of Israel could escape.

This Easter of ours commemorates the still more wonderful escape of the Lord Jesus Christ. By leaving this earth to return to heaven, he freed us from the tyranny of Satan and brought us to our true inheritance. Our Easter is that baptismal night of long ago when sinners escaped their doom at the moment Jesus left his tomb. Our Easter is the blood of the sacrificed Christ which won for us our salvation. The Paschal Lamb, of which the Israelites partook in a solemn act of thanksgiving for their deliverance, was merely symbolic of the "true Lamb" whose blood was to redeem us and who we receive in the Eucharist.

How can we restrain our joy? Christ has opened the gates of our prison. He has enabled us to pass from the field of our misery into the land of freedom. We were shipwrecked, doomed to the infernal depths, and as we fought the flood waters in futile effort, the hand of a dauntless ferryman grasped us and snatched us from the deep. The glorious result of his sacrifice was our passage from sin to love, from darkness to light, from death to life, from natural life subject to death to an endless supernatural life.

Are we completely freed from the slavery of sin? St. Paul's argument is conclusive. Death, he says, is the consequence, or "the wages" of sin; through the sin of one man death invaded the entire human race. But now, on Easter morning, sin has been destroyed. Since the punishment has been annulled, so the fault has been blotted out. As a consequence of Adam's disobedience we were dispossessed of the eternal intimacy for which God had destined us. We were reduced to remembering, in everlasting bitterness, our fallen state and regretting the paradise that we had lost forever. Death, which destroys our body as it withers the grass of the field, in the hands of Satan became a weapon for depriving us of these indescribable privileges with which God had favored us. No longer was heaven for men: the dream of life in God had gone.

But the Son of God, having become one of us, conquered invincible death by dying like one of us. He could have returned to glory by cheating death (as happened to Elias), but in that case he would have escaped death, and death would have retained its dominion over the rest of mankind. In order to *destroy* it, a man had to confront it, in order to loosen its hold and eradicate its sting.

*Mortem nostram destruxit.* Jesus "dismembered" our death: He divided it. The first death, the natural end of life, remains as the punishment for sin, but it is no more than a harmless passage leading into God's everlasting dwelling place. The second death, that of the damned, no longer affects those who have a part in Christ's resurrection.

Our Savior restored our life by rising again. He recovered for us the supernatural state in which God created us. We have once again become the adopted children of God. From now on we share the divine life of our risen brother. If we believe in him, if we adhere to his person under the sign of baptism, if we unite ourselves to him under the sign of the Eucharist, and if, acquiescing in his word, we put it into practice, then we form one body with him, "the Church of the risen."

We shall manifest this paschal joy, not only in our hymns of praise, but also in generous and determined efforts toward our own conversion. Yes, by his death Christ has freed us from sin, but on the condition that we do not allow sin to rule our bodies by yielding to its lusts. Let us offer ourselves to God,

St. Paul insists, as dead men returned to life: Let us place our bodies at God's service by making them the instruments of good works.

Our paschal joy ought to manifest itself in a display of brotherly love. That is the immediate response that Jesus expects in return for that proof of his love given to us on the morning of his resurrection. We show our gratitude and faith and preserve our purity more carefully by loving one another as brothers, as his brothers. "Holy Easter reveals itself to us today," runs a verse in the Byzantine liturgy: "Easter the immaculate, Easter the mighty, Easter of the believers, Easter that opens for us the gates of paradise."

# The Resurrection: Christianity's Foundation

*If Christ has not been raised, then our preaching is in vain*

*and your faith is in vain.*

−1 Corinthians 15:14

The joys and the hopes that Easter awakens in us owe their strength to one clear and established fact: Jesus Christ really did rise from the dead, and this is the basic fact of Christianity.

The apostles did not say to the world: "Hear the Gospel, for there is no more beautiful doctrine, nor any that better corresponds to the needs of man's reason and conscience. Its excellence and the unparalleled holiness of its author guarantee the truth of it." No, they did not preach a *doctrine* because it seemed true to them. They preached a *fact* of which they were certain. A doctrine may be debated, but a fact is indisputable. Reconsider the factual certainty of Easter, so that we may joyfully rely on the promises that it holds, and also courageously accept the effort that it calls forth in us.

On several occasions, either in parables or directly, Jesus told his disciples that he would be put to death in Jerusalem but would rise again on the third day; on each occasion his predictions were beyond their comprehension. After the Transfiguration, when Peter, James, and John had seen the manifestation of his divine glory, the Master had commanded them not to tell anybody until he had risen from the dead. The saying made little sense to them.

This uncertainty may still be found among the faithful today. In their eyes, the heaven into which Christ entered, body and soul, is scarcely distinguishable from that supra-terrestrial "beyond" where we locate the souls of the saints. They see little distinction between immortality and resurrection. Yet in saying that Jesus rose from the dead we mean something altogether different from the spiritual survival of our dead. It is the entire being of Jesus that returned to life. He who was dead is alive. Dying for us, he now lives with us; he is present in heaven and on earth. Until the end of the history of mankind, Jesus remains our contemporary.

If Jesus in his grave had submitted to the common fate, we should have regarded him as no more than one prophet among many, albeit the greatest. If his work had ended with the igno-minious death on the Cross, it would have ended in failure. To those who object that even had such been the case, Jesus would still have brought us a wonderful ideal of brotherhood and a unique example of holiness, we answer that it would do us no good beyond the present life. His intention in appearing is not only to show the apostles that he has freed himself from the bonds of death, but also that he is living that heavenly life which he promised to those who would believe in him. The risen Jesus appeared to the apostles in order to win their belief. On seeing him again, they understood that he would henceforth no longer be that Master who had traveled the roads of Galilee with them. Thomas was able to touch the Savior's wounds with his hand. Although Thomas believed only because of what he had just seen, what he believed surpassed what he actually saw. He "saw the man, and he confessed God," says St. Gregory.[1]

For us the resurrection of Jesus is the same. It is a fact that we accept because it contains the conditions normally required in order that an event be regarded as historically authentic. Moreover, it is a mystery demanding our credence, because of both the miraculous character of the fact and the supernatural realities it implies.

Christianity cannot have originated in the dreadful death of a man who was nailed to an infamous gibbet. Had the body of Jesus suffered the fate of all corpses, there would have been no Christianity. The faith of the disciples, most of whom were still looking for the messiah who would re-establish the nation of Israel in its former glory, would not have survived the terrible blow dealt to it by the shameful defeat of their Master. With Jesus dead, their ambition to establish the kingdom of God on earth would also be dead.

That they braved the Jewish and pagan authorities; that they dared to teach a moral doctrine that defies all the passions of men and insists on the most austere virtues in its adherents; that they dared to preach a religion that scandalized Jewish piety and was pure folly in the eyes of Greeks: All this was because Jesus had given them indisputable proof of his divinity by returning to speak to them after his death, to detail their mission and outline their apostolic program.

---

1   In Latin, *Hominem vidit, Deum confessus est*. St. Gregory the Great, *Homiliae in evangelia*, homily 26, n.8.

# WITNESSES OF THE RISEN SAVIOR

*God raised him on the third day and made him manifest;*

*not to all the people but to us who were chosen by God as*

*witnesses, who ate and drank with him after he rose from*

*the dead.*

—Acts 10:40–41

Twelve years elapsed before the primitive Church admitted a pagan into its fold. This follows an indication by the Lord that Peter, braving the scruples of his companions, should baptize the centurion Cornelius, the first pagan convert. This incident had such repercussions that St. Luke wrote about it in some detail. But the passage relating to the witnesses of the resurrection of Jesus requires some explanation.

St. Peter says, in effect, that God did not allow Jesus to show himself to all the people but only to a certain number chosen in advance; men who had formerly been his disciples and had eaten and drunk with him after his resurrection from the dead. This exclusiveness caused uneasiness in some circles, where it was regretted that proofs of the Resurrection had been granted only to a close group of friends. Would not open publicity have been better than this secrecy? People would have fallen to their knees on seeing the blood-stained Victim alive after death had claimed him. For this reason, the Savior did not allow them to see him after his resurrection. They were not prepared to believe.

On the other hand, to appear before all the astonished people would have been contrary to his character. Dramatic displays were not his way. Satan had suggested to him that he should show himself to be the Messiah by casting himself down from the pinnacle of the temple. The Savior was indignant at such a stratagem: He had not come to dazzle men but to convince them. He would not lead them to God by extraordinary paths but through unselfishness, humility, and love. He would not appeal to the eyes of the crowd but to the hearts of individuals. But even if the appearance of the risen Christ before the people of Jerusalem would have evoked more popular enthusiasm than Palm Sunday itself, how many of these tardy and superficial adherents would have understood the significance of such a marvel? What conclusion would they have drawn from so public a display? Without any doubt they would have seen it as the famed restoration of Israel that had been haunting the popular imagination. They would have instantly forgotten the Cross and the suffering. They would have been shocked once again by his refusal of the royal crown of David.

No, it was better that Jesus should not show himself to the people. His victory over death was not an act of political revenge upon those who had unjustly condemned him to be crucified, nor a marvel to inflame the minds of the people and divide them still more. Only the eyes of the humble, to whom the Father had revealed what the clever and the wise had missed, could behold Jesus whom God had sent. The Resurrection would be incomprehensible if it were detached from all the rest of the gospel, for it confirms what Jesus taught us about his person, his mission, and his work.

After more than two years spent beside his Master, Peter had come to know his completely spiritual character and the truly religious mission that God had assigned to the promised Messiah of Israel. Peter believed, and publicly confessed at Caesarea, that Jesus was the Messiah. When he recalled in memory all that he had known of the Savior, he recognized the impossibility of death claiming him as its victim. For he knew that Jesus was not a deified man, but God made man, the only Son come forth from the Father to enter this world. The resurrection of Jesus is the necessary consequence of his incarnation. Isolate the Resurrection from the earlier life of Jesus and it becomes something unnatural and nothing more. But relate it to the whole gospel and the Resurrection is seen to be its crowning point.

The Savior's whole teaching implied that his action would not be limited to the brief period of his preaching in Palestine. The kingdom of God which he came to inaugurate on earth would develop progressively there and would achieve its full flowering at the end of the world, when Christ will return in glory and majesty to judge the people of all nations. The disciples who remained faithful to Jesus until the hour of his death knew these basic principles of the kingdom of God and knew that he would go away and return again; the others did not know that. So it was right that the risen Christ should appear to them and not to the others.

The apostles learned from their Master that God wants to reign in men's hearts, transforming them gradually into the likeness of his Son, and that this transformation will be consummated in eternal life, for which his disciples must sacrifice this present life. The manifestation of the risen Savior to the masses would only have astonished them without being of any benefit to them.

The apostles instantly recognized that their Master's resurrection formed an integral part of the gospel they were to preach, to the extent that the Resurrection would be inconceivable without the rest of the gospel. As soon as the appearances had ceased, on the day after the Ascension, we find the disciples gathered in the upper room to choose someone to replace Judas. But they found only two men fit to rank in the apostolic college. Was it therefore not enough that the new apostle be one of those who has seen the risen Lord and so could testify to his divinity? The work of Jesus forms a whole which is indivisible. His resurrection is the last act of his mission, clarifying and justifying the completeness of that mission. The Cross and the Resurrection, closely welded to one another, form the key to all the secrets of the gospel.

Let us pray that the world, which is sliding so lamentably toward despair, may learn to look toward the tomb from which Jesus emerged on Easter morning. Let us pray that so many human hearts, hardened, abused, and discouraged, may discover our hope and want to share it with us. Assuredly we shall help them to be the faithful witnesses of the divine risen Lord, not only by the serene affirmation of our own faith, but above all by the hidden influence which a living faith exercises in its environment.

# THE RELIABILITY OF
# THE WITNESSES

*…[H]e had given commandment through the Holy
Spirit to the apostles whom he had chosen. To them he
presented himself alive after his passion by many proofs,
appearing to them during forty days, and speaking of the
kingdom of God.*

−Acts 1:2–3

The resurrection of Jesus is too important and too
far-reaching in its consequences for us not to be most
exacting about its proofs. Although the *sincerity* of the
witnesses cannot be honestly disputed, still it is not surprising to
find called into question the *objective reality* of the appearances.
Could the apostles have exteriorized a purely interior vision?

The story goes like this: The disciples of Jesus returned to
Galilee after the disappointment of Good Friday. There, in a
setting where everything spoke to them of the Master whom
they had not ceased to love, the memories of that promise-laden
epic haunted their minds, and little by little they reacted against
the appalling deception they had undergone. Then they understood the spiritual character of the kingdom of God as Jesus

had preached it, and which they had accepted with so much difficulty. They recalled the declarations that mystified them so greatly about the Son of Man who would rise again after being put to death; now they saw their meaning. Jesus was continuing to live; he was living in them. And since his tomb had been found empty two days after his burial, was that not proof that he was alive? Their discouragement was succeeded by a state of exaltation in which nothing would do but the belief that they had seen him—and so they affirmed their certainty of having seen him.

This psychological theory has been put forward with many variations. Its starting point is always a preconceived idea. When every supernatural event is rejected *a priori*, a natural explanation must be found for the birth and extension of Christianity, based as it is on the resurrection of Jesus.

The suspicion cast on the reliability of the disciples' affirmations needs to be considered. It is essential to show clearly that it does not stand up to the examination of the texts involved, which are the only ones to make known to us the origins of Christianity and the resurrection of the Savior. A text can be made to say many things—such is merely a matter of ingenuity—but it is more scientific to uncover what it actually says.

According to the explanation put forward, the apostles would appear to be visionaries. Now, hallucination suggests neurosis, and is an interior phenomenon by which a subject attributes reality to his fancies, desires, or fears. Everything we know about the apostles precludes the supposition that they were in such a state of mind. They were not neurotic hotheads but sound, level-headed men with their feet on the ground. If it is true that someone who suffers from hallucinations believes that he actually sees what in fact is only in his mind, then we may be reassured. The apostles professed the religious ideas of their time, and the Jews who believed in the resurrection of the just at the end of the world did not believe that any of them individually would rise again immediately after death.

In fact, in their grief, they so little expected the resurrection of Jesus that they regarded as foolish the women who first brought the news. Peter and John ran to the tomb and found it empty. That is where hallucination could possibly intervene. The two apostles looked carefully but could see no one. Neither they nor their companions had the idea yet of a messiah who would conquer death: He remained for them only a vanquished prophet abandoned by God.

Whereas a visionary does not question his visions but accepts them, the apostles did the opposite. They began to defend themselves against what they saw, which they could only describe as a "phantom." They distrusted themselves and feared that their eyes were deceiving them. Jesus spoke to them, and they could not believe what he said. They had to touch their Master's body, and those who did not have that experience refused to believe that he had risen.

The effect of surprise reoccurred at each new appearance. We find no instance of the disciples praying together with hopes of a vision. The Savior showed himself to them unexpectedly, when they were engaged in the most ordinary occupations, as they were traveling, or at the end of a meal or returning from fishing. Individual, isolated visions could have led to caution, but most of the appearances had several witnesses, and all saw the same thing at the same moment. Two, seven, eleven people—once as many as five hundred—saw him.

It is equally unheard of that a person subject to hallucination should persist in that state: Either his illness will get worse until he finally falls into a state of mental derangement, or he may be cured of his trouble, in which case it is painful for him even to allude to the alleged visions that he now recognizes as unbalanced. How different was the attitude of the disciples who saw the risen Savior! Right up to the end of their lives they remained unanimously and unshakably loyal to their certainty. Not even one retracted, not one uttered a doubt about Jesus' rising from the dead.

None of the arguments that we have just put forward is the fruit of a tendentious interpretation of the texts under discussion. They reflect exactly the general view of an unprejudiced reader. Would a more searching inquiry be less conclusive? Let us put it to the test.

People seem amazed that the four Gospels do not contain the same unique account of the appearances. But indeed, what a lot of objections there would be if the four writers (who each followed a particular plan and wrote for a different milieu) had suddenly reproduced the same stereotyped account in each Gospel!

In the first place our Gospels would never have been written if their authors had not been certain about the resurrection of Jesus. It was not their intention to prove the fact of the resurrection of Jesus to those who might doubt it. They affirmed the fact, which is a fundamental certainty of the Church, the crowning point of the earthly mission of Jesus and the conclusive proof of his divinity. So they did not deem it necessary to enumerate all the appearances known to them and to all Christians. They made their choice from the appearances in the way they did from incidents, journeys, miracles, and teachings that they related from the ministry of Jesus. What justification is there for claiming that Matthew was unaware of the parable of the Good Samaritan because it does not appear in his book; and can we quibble with Luke for omitting the parable of the unjust steward, which appears only in Matthew? It would be no less arbitrary to suggest that each of the four narrators knew only of the appearances which feature in his own writings.

Fixing dates and mentioning certain particularities were of very little importance to the first preachers, and consequently to the evangelists, in comparison with the tremendous fact that had suddenly burst upon the former disciples of the Savior. A carefully arranged setting and strict chronology would give rise to a suspicion different from any suggested by the pages of the Gospels, in which we find extensive accounts side by side with hurried notes and immediate impressions. This lack of preparation gives the feeling that we are listening to eyewitnesses.

In conclusion, two points merit consideration. First, the Savior showed himself to his disciples during the forty days following his resurrection, after which none of them was to see him again (except the special case of St. Paul). The second point is no less conclusive. The invented psychological reconstructions try to persuade us that, on returning from Galilee, the loyalty and devotion of the disciples to the Savior led them to believe in his survival. But Jesus began to show himself in Jerusalem on the *third* day after his death. Far from a purely subjective faith having led the apostles to believe that they had seen Jesus appear to them in his own flesh, it was, on the contrary, his quick return to their midst and his repeated appearances that created and consolidated their faith. It was only after they had seen, touched, and heard him that they grasped what the Savior meant when he spoke to them about his resurrection from the dead.

It was only because Jesus spoke to them several times at

length about the realities of the kingdom of God that they began to abandon their illusions about an earthly messiah and to understand that the kingdom of God on earth would be achieved in that glory to which Christ was going before them and where his disciples would be reunited with him. Only then did the apostles appreciate, in all its overwhelming reality, the unheard-of privilege which they had enjoyed in living for three years in the closest intimacy with the Son of God.

We can therefore accept their testimony with complete assurance without scrutinizing the Gospel texts in an inquisitorial manner. We will not be seeking the mere satisfaction of historical reconstruction. Each account contains a lesson that will reveal to us the inexhaustible riches of the Easter mystery and will guide our footsteps in the new life into which the risen Christ has brought us.

# AT DAWN ON THE THIRD DAY

*And they were saying to one another, "Who will roll away the stone for us from the door of the tomb?"*

–Mark 16:3

The Lord predicted that the apostles would all abandon him in the hour of trial. They were effectively dispersed all over the city during Friday's tragic events. We cannot imagine that in their state of desolation they would have gathered, either in the upper room or elsewhere. What would there have been to bring them together? Their pain and their shame were too acute, and moreover they had good reason to fear that the Jewish authorities, after their triumph, might lay hands on them. It was wiser not to attract attention to themselves. Thanks to the numbers of pilgrims staying in Jerusalem and the neighborhood during the paschal festivities, they could move about unnoticed, and there were some friendly households to offer them a safe refuge.

We know that John had taken Jesus' mother with him. Peter had good reasons for wanting to be left alone with his remorse and misery. He was alone when Jesus appeared to him during the daytime on Sunday, and when Mary Magdalen saw the tomb empty, she ran first to him and then to the other disciple whom Jesus loved. The apostle Thomas was not to be found on the Sunday evening when the eleven decided to meet. The holy women must also have kept apart. This dispersion of the Savior's friends in the city's crowded streets accounts for the comings and goings between Jerusalem and the tomb on Golgotha.

Shortly after the burial of Jesus the first lamps of the Sabbath were lit. Nobody would have dared infringe the strict precept of rest. It was not until Saturday that the holy women were able to procure the spices and perfumed oils needed for anointing the Savior's body to complete Friday's hasty embalming. Exactly how many holy women were there? At least six and very probably more. All four accounts mention Mary Magdalen. They left the city in little groups while it was still dark in order to reach Joseph of Arimathea's garden at sunrise.

Not one suspected what awaited them. The jars of perfume they were bringing indicate clearly enough that they were going to anoint his body as a last token of their love. But one thing worried them: They had seen the place on the previous evening, including the large stone that closed the tomb entrance. They wondered if they would find anyone at that hour to roll back this heavy stone in its groove.

How many times had Jesus counseled them not to give way to anxiety! Things rarely turn out as we fear. We get lost in suppositions and precautions, and the result often turns out quite unlike what we had foreseen. So it is simpler to leave everything to God. The holy women were about to have this proof, for when they came near the tomb, the stone had already been rolled away.

A key point should be mentioned here. The Evangelists tell us of the risen Jesus, but not one of them elaborates on the actual resurrection itself. A forger would not have failed to describe this wonder in detail, and indeed some apocryphal versions ventured to do so later on. The Evangelists themselves only report what the disciples saw. They leave our curiosity unsatisfied as to what may have happened when no witnesses were present. This strict reserve is a valuable guarantee of their veracity. The tomb was found empty at dawn on the third day—this fact has been duly recorded—but nobody saw Jesus emerge.

St. Matthew took down the version given by the Jewish authorities immediately after the astounding event, and he repeated it when he wrote his Gospel. The Sanhedrin, after deliberation, bribed the guards and charged them to spread the official explanation of a stolen body. In fact the guards, suddenly awakened by an earthquake, had seen the stone overturned and the tomb empty. Afraid, they fled in all haste to make their report to the high priests.

Too much editorial treatment of the first Evangelist does not leave it clear beyond dispute whether he says the soldiers saw the angel or whether its appearance was reserved for the women. This second interpretation conforms with the more circumstantial accounts of Mark and Luke. The latter depict the fear of the holy women at the empty tomb. Could someone have desecrated the Master's grave? The thought of incurring such a reproach would cause great offense to the mind of a pious Jew. While the little group remained perplexed, Mary Magdalen thought of telling Peter and John as soon as she could. She ran from the garden to go and tell them. Had she seen the angel she would certainly have stayed with the others.

None of the women thought of the possibility of a resurrection. Having recovered from their bewilderment, some of them ventured to enter the tomb that had been hewn out of the rock. Right at the back, they saw the stone ledge on which the Savior's body had been laid. They had hardly emerged when the Lord revealed the incredible truth.

Differences appear in the Evangelists' accounts. "While they were perplexed about this, behold, two men stood by them in dazzling apparel" (Lk 24:4). Mark and Matthew mention only one person: "a young man sitting on the right side, dressed in a white robe" (Mk 16:5). "[A]n angel of the Lord descended from heaven and came and rolled back the stone, and sat upon it. His appearance was like lightning, and his raiment white as snow" (Mt 28:2–4). The basic facts correspond in all three accounts. It would have been unusual if the stories of the witnesses, handed down by word of mouth, had not shown some variations, none of which affect the fundamental authenticity of the event.

"He is not here. He is risen." This statement features in all the accounts. Luke's text takes on a special solemnity: "'Why do you seek the living among the dead? He is not here, but has risen. Remember how he told you, while he was still in Galilee, that the Son of man must be delivered into the hands of sinful men, and be crucified, and on the third day rise.' And they remembered his words" (Lk 24:5–8). The accounts given by Mark and Matthew are almost the same.

These Galilean women well deserved to be the first to know about the Easter victory. For month after month, keeping discreetly in the background, they had ministered to the needs of the disciples who were accompanying Jesus. Although they took no part in the discussions in which the men were so passionately involved, their devotion found its reward in the teachings that Jesus kept for his closest friends. And because they humbly received his words, they were perhaps better prepared than the apostles for the appalling tragedy of Calvary.

Another woman, Mary of Bethany, who did not belong to their group, must have had some foreboding a few days before the catastrophe, when she poured a vase of spices on his head, as was done for the dead. The women of Galilee had certainly been overwhelmed, as the apostles were, when they saw that God had not saved from death the one whom they had regarded as his messiah and who called himself his son. However, they wept above all else because they had lost him.

Women are, as a rule, more religious than men, but this does not derive solely from the greater depth of feeling they manifest in the expression of their faith. The cause is deeper than that: their faith is primarily loyalty, faithfulness. They reason just as much as men do, though in a different way, and their intuition leads them to the heart of the mystery before men's considered deductions. They too traverse regions of obscurity and doubt, but with a firmer tread, because their whole being is given to God in their act of faith. They also have the ability to wait. Where a man cuts through a knot with a knife, a woman patiently unties it. They accept the incomprehensible slings of adversity more courageously than men do; they know that in great adversity the last word is not spoken and that only God will speak it. Their trust is more interior and purer, and they usually end up being right, without knowing why.

So while the disciples—except for John, who had not left Mary—were somberly reflecting on their betrayal and their grief and concluding that there was nothing more to be done, the women of Galilee thought that they could still do something. At least they could make a loving gesture to honor the burial place of Jesus. They obeyed the dictates of their loyalty. It was only on the way that they realized their great fear: They lacked a tool to move the heavy stone. And because they had been the most eager, it was they to whom Jesus gave the good news that he was not to be sought among the dead.

The angels vanished, the stone lay on the ground, the tomb, empty. Were their troubles over? They had yet to roll away another stone, a much heavier one, and one that daunts the best of men in their efforts to believe. They were now commanded to find his disciples. Nothing more effectively helps to smooth away inner worries than the performance of some physical act. The control that we must then exercise over our body gives us greater control over our thoughts. The little group decides to break up before setting out for Jerusalem. It is now broad daylight; they must not arouse the suspicions of passersby who would be intrigued at seeing all these women carrying sachets of spices and jars of perfumes. However anxious they were to hasten their mission, prudence suggested that they should scatter, taking different roads on the way back to the city.

That fact emerges from the Evangelists' description. Mark tells us of a little group of women, so frightened and stunned when they got back to the city that their speech and their breath failed them (Mk 16:8). Matthew, with his usual precision, also portrays the messengers as being terrified but at the same time filled with joy. They waste no time in bringing the news to the disciples (Mt 28:8). It will be remembered that, before the angelic intervention, Mary Magdalen ran from the garden to look for Peter and John, but when these eventually arrived at the tomb the holy women had gone. They were already going around the streets of Jerusalem, but having failed to find the

*mindful breaths*

two chief apostles, they decided instead to join some of the
eleven and other disciples. At that hour of day pilgrims were
converging in a crowd toward the temple. Reading between
the lines of St. Luke's account suggests that the women drew
the disciples apart to give them the message they had brought,
and that Jesus' friends were meeting together here and there
to discuss the strange tidings. What the Evangelist does not
in any way conceal from us is the reception that the disciples
gave to the women's stories: "[B]ut these words seemed to
them an idle tale, and they did not believe them" (Lk 24:11).

The disciples' confusion of mind excuses them, in our eyes,
for disregarding the women's accounts. What disconcerted
them most of all was the disappearance of Jesus' body. They
imagined this to have been a final piece of spite on the part of
his enemies, who wanted to deprive him of a tomb that was too
splendid for a criminal. It was urgent that they should find out
where he had been taken. As for the stories about angels that
the women were telling at once, that was considered delirium.
Their state of excitement would be enough to make their stories
suspect. By refusing to credit their tales, the apostles and the
disciples at least showed they were far from supposing that the
Savior must rise from the dead. Their initial refusal to believe
is our guarantee of the objectivity and reality of the evidence
they will later bring to light.

# Peter and John at the Tomb

*Peter then came out with the other disciple, and they went*

*toward the tomb.*

–John 20:3

Faced with the disappearance of the body, the closest friends of Jesus first envisaged the most natural explanation, a surreptitious removal, instead of immediately exclaiming it as something miraculous. This is also the point beyond which those who deny the supernatural have refused to go. Rather than admit to a miracle, they have imagined the most fantastic hypotheses where the plain reading of the text allows none.

Some have attributed the "removal" to the followers of Jesus, who would have wanted it to be believed that he had risen. Proper judgment has long since disposed of this imputation of treachery. That the apostles should have based the faith and the preaching of their whole lives on an imposture is a pitiable suggestion, as is giving credence to the petty conspiracy devised by the high priests. The attitude of the Sanhedrin showed quite plainly that the body had disappeared on the morning of the third day and that they did not know how it had happened.

Supporters of the removal theory have nevertheless pre-

ferred to attribute the initiative to the enemies of Jesus. The
authorities, we are told, had an interest in making the body
disappear. This tomb, besides being too respectable for a man
who had been crucified, was in danger of becoming a place of
pilgrimage for his disciples. In addition, the miracle of tongues
on the day of Pentecost, and afterward the healing of the cripple
at the temple gate, had aroused a great stir in the holy city.
Already five thousand men had embraced the new faith. The
Sanhedrin decided to summon the apostles to appear before its
court, where Peter charged the chief priests with Jesus' death,
whereas God had raised him from death. Faced with such a
categorical declaration, the magistrates could do no more than
threaten the apostles, warning them not to continue speaking
about Jesus. They said nothing because they did not know why
the body was no longer in the tomb. Neither the enemies of
Jesus nor his friends had removed it.

Let us go back to the first hours of Easter Sunday; the actual
dispositions of the witnesses are more interesting than the most
subtle suppositions. St. John's memories are precise; he had
recounted them many times before writing them down in his
Gospel. At the news that the tomb was empty, Peter and he
had run there; he, being younger and quicker, was the first to
reach the garden. Without going into the tomb, he bent down
as far as the opening beneath the funeral chamber and noticed
the linen bands lying on the ground.

When Simon Peter arrived, he did not hesitate to go right
inside the tomb. As well as the bands lying on the ground he
saw, at some distance, the linen cloth which had been placed at
the head of the body. The continuation of the account implies
that the two apostles immediately concluded that the body had
not been taken away. Vandals would have taken it as it was,

without spending time unwrapping the linen cloths that bound it and carefully folding the napkin that covered the face. The body had not been removed. What then is the explanation?

John does not reveal the thoughts of his companion, for the latter was deep in silence. St. Luke, who also mentions Simon Peter's race to the tomb, says that the apostle, having seen the linen cloths, returned to his own home, *secum mirans,* "wondering to himself" what could have happened. Despite his weakness and his unworthiness, he had a mission to fulfill toward the other apostles, for he was still their leader with a duty to enlighten and guide them. Hence, we can understand his reserve. He was not aware of the angel's intervention, nor the message of the women. He knew only one thing: The tomb was empty, though the body had not been taken away. Peter remained alone and prayed. In the evening the disciples were to learn that he had seen the Lord. Henceforth Peter will begin to confirm his brethren in the faith.

The apostle John likewise returned whence he came, respectful of Peter's silence. Although John said nothing, he had already penetrated the mystery of the inexplicable disappearance.

It would be essential that the infant Church, and her members for generations to come, have some clear and indisputable witnesses to the Resurrection. That is why we are indebted to Peter for not having spoken before he had seen the Lord. The resistance of the eleven and of the other disciples to the women's stories, their discussions in the Upper Room, and the obstinate refusal to believe guarantee to us that the faith of the Church is not due to the blind enthusiasm of the first men who were loyal to Jesus. Our faith would be in danger of wavering were it not based on the foundations of strict certainty. Peter is right in making us wait, but John is not wrong in showing us that faith springs from love. In this regard, could there be an additional reason for the rapidity of John's faith? Jesus had given something more than the sacrament of his Body and Blood to the disciple whom he loved. The crucified Lord had also asked Mary to look on John as her son and had entrusted his holy mother to him. Did Mary and John merely weep and pray together, from Friday evening until Sunday morning, without exchanging any conversation? Would it surprise us if Mary, anticipating the role which she was to play in the Church, had, during that time, been guiding the apostle's faith toward the reality that was to come? Might she not have reminded him of the assurance of resurrection that her Son had given them?

Catholic piety requires us to believe that the Blessed Virgin was the first to whom the risen Savior showed himself, although there is no mention of this fact in the Gospels. Of one thing we can be certain: Mary was expecting that hour of triumph, because her faith had never wavered.

*how can you know this.*

# MEETING MARY MAGDALEN

*Jesus said to her, "Mary." She turned and said to him in Hebrew, "Rab-bo'ni!" (which means Teacher).*

–John 20:16

The fourth Gospel gives a detailed account of the Lord's appearance to Mary Magdalen. This had already been mentioned in the closing lines of St. Mark's account. Having risen on the morning of the third day, Jesus appeared first to Mary Magdalen, the woman out of whom he had cast seven devils. This incident needs clarification. This faithful servant of Jesus is similarly described by St. Luke when he introduces her. Among the women were some he had freed from evil spirits and from sickness, Mary Magdalen, Joanna, the wife of Chuza, who was Herod's steward, and Susanna, and many others who ministered to him with their own means. These women did not form a composite group, as did the twelve; they merely followed Jesus and the apostles in their journeyings in order to minister to their material needs, with great reserve and delicacy. These women, some of whom were of quite exalted social rank, showed in this way their appreciation to the Savior who had cured them of disease or freed them from diabolical possession. *all walks of life*

Mary Magdalen belonged to the latter category. The expression "seven devils," equivalent to a multitude of devils, suggests that the unfortunate woman had been the object of a singularly vicious possession. The miracle that delivered her from this terrible condition gave her a certain measure of renown as the recipient of a special favor. It will be noticed, as well, that the women who thus dedicated themselves to the cause of the gospel had been sick or possessed, but not one of them had lived in sin. The implication of sin arises from the tendency to regard those possessed by devils as wretches subject to every vice. A possessed person can also be a sinner, but possession does not require falling into sin. To assume that Mary Magdalen had previously led a bad life makes an inference that is difficult to accept and has no support in any of the Gospels.

A tradition in the Latin Church held that Mary Magdalen, Mary of Bethany (the sister of Lazarus), and the pardoned sinner were the same person. This identification, adopted by St. Gregory the Great, is still accredited by the presence in the Roman calendar of the feast of St. Mary Magdalen, Penitent, on July 22. The Greek Fathers did not subscribe to this tradition, and it was also rejected by the great Latin doctors Ambrose, Hilary, Jerome, and Bede. Each of the three women has a separate feast day in the Eastern liturgies. St. Luke, who alone mentions all three, does not establish any connections between them. Let us be content to see only her whom the Byzantines call the "myrrh-bearer," who ranks in stature with the apostles, whom the mercy of Jesus had delivered only from one of the most humiliating of afflictions. She, in return, offered him all her love and devotion, meriting thereby the great privilege of seeing the risen Lord even before the apostles. Mary Magdalen was not among the "witnesses chosen beforehand" to be the official preachers of the Resurrection. Although the Lord charged her to notify his disciples, the favor he conferred on her by appearing to her before he showed himself to them takes on a personal character; above all it was a reward for her loyalty. Moreover, we may examine the plain facts of the Gospels, which make it sufficiently clear that Magdalen had no hallucinations and that it was not she who determined the faith of the apostles.

When Peter and John hurried to the tomb, she had evidently been unable to keep up with them. Although she quickened her pace, she joined them only after they had seen the state of the tomb. We have seen how they withdrew; John not daring to express his belief, Peter absorbed in his thoughts. Their silence only succeeded in increasing Mary Magdalen's uncertainty, for she was still unaware of the revelation made to her female companions by the angel. So she allowed the two apostles to go away—they had no further need of her—and she remained behind. Alone, she gave full rein to her grief. This tomb had sheltered the body of her Master, who had freed her from Satan's stranglehold. Of her beloved Master, whom she had lost, nothing remained. So she wept before the empty tomb.

There was nobody in the garden, nobody to stop her going to the stone on which Jesus had lain and touching it with her hand. Still weeping, she bent down to look inside the tomb.. Two figures clothed in white had entered unobserved before her; they stood at either end of the bier. Later she would remember them as angels, but for the moment her thoughts were elsewhere. They said to her, "Woman, why are you weeping?" Let us listen to the reply of the woman whom some would like to dismiss as a visionary. She was far removed from supposing that Jesus might have risen. She was entirely convinced that the tomb had been robbed. Instinctively, she shrank back and left the tomb. Who were these men who had spoken to her? Her eyes now beheld another unknown person, whose face meant nothing to her. Possibly it was a servant who looked after Joseph of Arimathea's garden. Like the others, he seemed surprised at the presence of a woman sobbing there. "[W]hy are you weeping?' he asked her (Jn 20:15). The so-called visionary did not lose her head; calmly she pursued her thought. Perhaps this "servant" could enlighten her. "Sir, if you have carried him away, tell me where you have laid him, and I will take him away" (Jn 20:15).

Here we have the first instance of a unique quality of the risen body of Jesus. Not only did the Savior suddenly appear whenever he wished, but he also allowed himself to be recognized or not, at will. The new life into which he had entered is in no way comparable to our earthly condition. St. John Chrysostom thought that by hiding the features which Mary would have recognized, Jesus had wanted to spare her a sudden violent shock. In any case, we are certain that she did not for a moment imagine that Jesus could show himself to her.

The unknown man who surprised her could only be the gardener, she thought. She was not expecting a miracle of any sort. She was moved, and we should be surprised if she had not been, but she did not appear over-excited. Her generous nature is revealed in her intention to carry away the body by herself if someone would only tell her where to find it. She had been worried, as her companions had been, about being able to roll away the heavy stone that had sealed the tomb; now she was ready to carry a weight that far exceeded her strength. She was little concerned with the gardener himself, constantly directing her gaze toward the inside of the tomb. Upon hearing hear name, "Mary," she turned toward her questioner.

Now she could not mistake the voice or the tones of the speaker. That was how the Savior had addressed her every day. Now it was indeed the Master's face that she saw before her eyes, and she replied to him with *Rabboni*, a more intimate form than the word *Rabbi*, which the disciples used.

She threw herself at his feet and embraced him. But for Mary, what has gone before is not to begin again. The time has not yet come for the everlasting joys of the Father's house. She did not go into ecstasies. Ever obedient to his wishes, she did not try to prolong this moment of intimacy. The Master has not yet ascended; he has not yet left our world. Peter, John, and the others still have some chance of seeing him again. Jesus had shown himself to her; would he not show himself to them also? The surroundings of the tomb were again deserted; Mary Magdalen hurried toward Jerusalem.

John's account is limited to telling us that she fulfilled her mission. Mark is more explicit: "She went out and told those who had been with him, as they mourned and wept. But when they heard that he was alive and had been seen by her, they would not believe it" (Mk 16:10–11). We must not be unsympathetic to their grief. The women's stories had left them skeptical; the disappearance of the body had only plunged them into even greater desolation.

We must not conclude, however, that they were ready to seize upon the first indication that might deliver them from their desolation. Their pain cannot be denied, but facts remain facts. For them to believe that Jesus was alive, certain proofs would be necessary; not mere hearsay, even if it were attributed to angels, nor even the report that Mary Magdalen had just given. The episode of Mary Magdalen at the tomb is inscribed forever in the religious history of souls; it sounds as a rallying

*I never thought of MM as an inspirational figure*

cry for Christians who suddenly find that they can no longer believe. The Lord they were acquainted with has disappeared, and they do not know where to look for him. Such people who struggle amidst doubts and denials should look to Mary Magdalen, for she will show them a sure road along which they cannot lose their way. She will invite them to continue to love Jesus Christ whatever may happen to them.

Perhaps you can no longer see him? Is there nothing before you but the yawning gap of your vanished and seemingly irreplaceable beliefs? Yet be sure that he sees you and he is near you, though you do not recognize him. No one can say how long your trial will last, but be assured that if you regret not seeing him, you will one day hear his voice calling your name.

To steadfast believers also, the devoted loyalty of Mary Magdalen should serve as a model, saving them from crises of conscience that might jeopardize their faith. The faith that dies is the faith which no longer searches, which flinches in the face of difficulties, which is not prepared to fight to survive. The faith in danger of death is the faith which is shut away in a corner of the mind so that it does not trouble the heart, whose only sustenance is inactive, empty piety which is allowed to lie dormant. On the other hand, a living faith gives us no rest. The Lord tells each of us to return to our brethren. Do not become impatient with those whom you do not convince at once, or those who may even accuse you of madness or malice. Let them see your faith by letting them share your joy. When their eyes will eventually recognize him is not your concern. Tell them simply: I have met the Lord and this is what he told me.

# WITH THE DISCIPLES
# IN EMMAUS

*"Did not our hearts burn within us while he talked with us on the road, while he opened to us the scriptures?"*

–Luke 24:32

St. Luke spent two years in Caesarea, where St. Paul had been imprisoned, so he knew the road joining Jaffa with Jerusalem via the market town of Emmaus. He undoubtedly stopped there to meet Cleophas, for we can detect firsthand information in his account of the apparition.

Cleophas and his friend faithfully represent the disciples' state of mind during the first part of Sunday morning. When the two left the city nothing was yet known about the appearance to Mary Magdalen. If they had been told about it, Cleophas and his companion would probably have postponed their departure. What had already happened had certainly astounded them: the disappearance of the body, confirmed by Peter and John, and the declarations of the Galilean women that angels had told them Jesus was alive. They had grounds for being disturbed. Yet they still did not suspect the truth.

The idea that his body might have returned to life struck them as absurd, for after all, nobody had seen Jesus—neither the women, nor Peter, nor John. The rest seemed to them to complicate a matter that was already obscure enough. In those circumstances, what was the point of remaining in Jerusalem any longer, where everybody was discussing "the affair of Jesus of Nazareth"? Cleophas and his unnamed friend were among the first to go. In six hours they would be home in Emmaus, where they would try to forget.

But would they ever forget? The two travelers were unable to shake off their unhappiness on the way. They were thinking only of Jesus; it was only of him that they spoke. And he whom they thought dead suddenly joined them at a bend in the road. But like Mary Magdalen outside the tomb, they did not recognize him.

Jesus caught up with them and joined their conversation, asking them to explain why they were so upset. Cleophas upbraided the ignorance of their new companion, telling him what had happened over the last few days, and how Jesus' death had dashed their hopes. Jesus listened without interrupting; he let his fellow travelers pour out their disappointments. "But we had hoped that he was the one to redeem Israel" (Lk 24:21). And all the joy and enthusiasm contained in that hope had now given way to bitter disappointment. "We *had* hoped." That hope is now gone; it was a grave mistake.

What was this hope they had entertained right up to the last minute? The very thing which Jesus had never promised them, and toward which he had constantly discouraged their ambitions. They had expected a militant messiah, leader of a theocratic kingdom who, after freeing Israel from the Roman yoke, would have ruled all nations under the banner of the one true God. It was for this reason that Jesus walked with Cleophas and his companion beneath the hot morning sun without revealing his identity to them. He hid himself from

their eyes so that their minds, slow to understand the Scriptures, might not be distracted from the truth they had to learn.
His revelation of the divine plan stirred their hearts while it
illuminated their understanding. They had lost all count of
time and any feelings of weariness and were surprised to find
Emmaus already in sight. No doubt but that the two disciples
were trying to guess his identity. The authority of his speech
doubtless restrained them from asking. Yet they surely did not
fail to wonder about this teacher who was so well versed in
the Scriptures, and whose explanations fitted in so remarkably
well with current events. But this coincidence did not for
the moment suggest to them that their traveling companion
might be Jesus himself. So far were they from expecting his
resurrection that when they reached Emmaus they still had no
suspicion of the identity of this pilgrim.

The journey had seemed short to them, for they had not
tired of listening to their unknown friend. He was making
as if to continue on his way, but could he not be persuaded
to stay with them? The excuse put forward by Cleophas was
weak enough: The sun was beginning to set and the traveler
still had to cover a good distance. The real motive, which was
to prevail over the mysterious traveler's hesitation, was the call
of friendship—the appeal of a shipwrecked man to the hand
that will drag him from the deep: "Stay with us."

So he joined them. Who, then, invented the curious legend
of the "inn" at Emmaus? Cleophas and his companion had
their house in Emmaus; perhaps they even lived under the
same roof. Luke makes no mention of an inn at all. Cleophas
joyfully brings Jesus into his house, doubtless in the hope that
he will stay there if possible. After their tiring journey the
travelers are eager to begin the improvised meal set out on

the family table. Being mid-afternoon, the other inhabitants of the house are still outside working; only the three are in the room. Here, then, Jesus prepares to reveal himself to them by a simple gesture, without uttering a word, for he has already told them in words what he wished them to learn.

It was Cleophas' duty, as head of the house, to break the bread and offer it to his guest. However, a curious reversal of custom takes place, for the guest takes bread into his hands as though it were he who had invited them. It is he who, acting with authority, recites the prayer of blessing as though he were master of the house. And here he is breaking the bread in the same way as the two disciples had first seen him do it in their midst. Why should Jesus still disguise himself from them? The Master! It is indeed he. Then they recognize him, and he disappears from sight.

Leaving the meal untouched, they immediately head back to Jerusalem. Now they had something more to think about than eating and resting. They had to get back to their friends who were still grieving in Jerusalem and tell them that Jesus was alive. When they got back to the holy city the night was dark, but they knew where to find them. Breathless and deeply moved as they were, those to whom they first spoke refused to take them seriously and continued to be incredulous. Unperturbed, they search for the apostles, and another surprise awaits them: the news that the Lord had appeared to Simon. Peter confirmed the news, and Cleophas and his companion began to tell the others what had happened to them on the road, and how they had recognized him in the breaking of the bread.

Whether we are eating, or drinking, or whatever we are doing, we remain the adopted children of God in all our activities. The Lord comes among us when we ask him. He is always on our road, though our eyes may be prevented from seeing him. If he is silent, it is because we are forgetting him; he only awaits a sign from us to explain the words of Scripture, enlightening our minds and warming our hearts.

How happy are they who speak to him every day, who thank him for his gifts, who ask for his guidance before they act, who invoke him in their every action. Jesus is our constant companion. In days of gladness, he sanctifies our joys, making them richer and glorifying the Father through the good works that we perform under his influence and in his name. And in times of suffering, he draws us to himself in a distinct way. If only we turned to him at once, our sorrows would be less heavy to bear. In truth, we cease to hope only when we cease to think that he is near us.

We sometimes allow ourselves to be saddened because experience, we think, brings contradictions to our faith. We had hoped that Christ would change our life, but we invariably find ourselves mediocre believers and attracted toward sin. We had hoped that Christianity would transform the world, but humanity always seems to draw away from it, to become more wicked and to stagger headlong, like a blind man, toward worse evils. "We had hoped." In reality we follow our own human judgment, and it is we who are at fault.

Stay with us, Lord, for the day is far spent. The years are passing and soon our pilgrimage will end. We are so far from holiness, we have done so little good here below, we have loved you so badly. Stay with us and help us achieve what we have failed to do and what, unaided, we shall ever fail to do: to become one with you. Take us by the hand in the hour of death—that vital journey by which you will bring us to the divine glory of the Resurrection.

# THE EVENING
# OF THE THIRD DAY

*"See my hands and my feet, that it is I myself; handle*
*me, and see; for a spirit has not flesh and bones as you*
*see that I have."*

–Luke 24:39

The first appearances of Jesus to Mary Magdalen and to Peter were intended to condition the minds of the disciples to the idea—to them a preposterous one—of his resurrection. Now he was going to put an end to their uncertainty by appearing to all of them together.

Very probably, after seeing the Lord, Simon Peter sent word to the eleven to assemble together at nightfall; the invitation reached all except Thomas. According to Luke, some companions had joined them, as generally supposed at the house where they had celebrated the Passover. They felt that in meeting together they were guilty of grave imprudence. The Jewish authorities, aware of the empty tomb, must have attributed the disappearance of the body to his disciples; they might already be looking for the suspected culprits. What a masterly scoop it would be for them to discover the disciples all here together. And so the door of the supper room was bolted. A knock on the door came as the disciples had just completed their meal. Their agitation soon vanished; it was not the agents of the Sanhedrin, but Cleophas and his friend, who confirmed the amazing news which Peter had announced: The Lord was alive!

They were still speaking when Jesus himself appeared in their midst, though all the doors were closed. "Peace be with you." All of them recognized the Master's familiar words: the joyful greeting which he gave them every morning and the same words with which he bade them goodnight. But was it really he speaking to them, as though nothing had happened? Stupefied with fear, they thought that it was an apparition.

The word *apparition* should here be given the meaning of ghost, a phantom or specter, some image recalling the person who has died. In short, the apostles had anticipated the skeptics of later ages by thinking in terms of an hallucination. An instinctive reaction made them think that they were victims of an illusion, and made them reject the physical reality of he who stood in their midst.

But Jesus had not lost the habit of reading his disciples' thoughts: "What," he said to them, "are you dismayed? Be assured that it is myself." Then the Lord lent himself to a most minute examination. They crowded around him to look at his hands and his feet, where the wounds of the Crucifixion were clearly visible. They inspected his side, which bore the mark of the wound made by the spear. But, lest their eyes should deceive them, to touch him would be more convincing.

Yet they still hesitated. They mistrusted the joy that they were experiencing at seeing him again; it was too good to be true. But Jesus persevered. He asked them for something to eat. They offered him a piece of roast fish, which he took and ate in their sight. If we wanted proof that Jesus was not a spirit, here it was. How could a body that had passed into the state of glory absorb material food, and what could happen to the piece of fish that he ate? Here we find ourselves in the realm of the miraculous, no less than when he multiplied the bread and fish to feed the multitude. It is one of those aspects of the Resurrection which, as we have already said, requires the submission of faith. His purpose was to assure them that they were not suffering from hallucinations, that they were in the presence of a fact. He had not assumed a bodily form to appear to them, but had taken on his former body, the same body with which he had walked, talked, and eaten with them. Henceforth his body had other properties (he had no need to use the door to come among them), because he had entered the glorious life that God has destined for all.

The historical truth of the gospel narrative strikes us once again in the way it relates the happiness of the first witnesses of the Resurrection. No excessive demonstrations were needed; their joy was interior, for what they had experienced defied all expression. In the space of a few days the cause to which they had devoted their lives had suffered total defeat, and when it had seemed irretrievably lost, he had reappeared to them.

The Resurrection is a most obscure phenomenon. Yes, it was indeed he, but why had he submitted to death? The Lord was not going to leave them in suspense. He instructs them to teach all nations that pardon of sins was to be granted in his name to all who accepted the evangelical message of salvation. These two themes are closely related. Sins could be pardoned only because Jesus had expiated all the sins of the world, and the exclusively religious character of the kingdom of God was confirmed by his resurrection. The apostles now knew that the work of Jesus had not ended, that it would continue by *did they really know they were creating a priesthood?*

means of their priesthood. The same gift from heaven that had brought the Incarnation to the world would also bequeath to it the Church. As the Father had sent his only Son, so was that Son now sending them to every nation on the same mission of salvation, whose primary function was the remission of sins.

On the evening of his resurrection, he expressly conferred on them the divine prerogative of forgiving sins, not only to declare them to be remitted by the sacrifice of the Cross, but to apply that redemptive sacrifice to men and judge whether forgiveness ought to be granted or refused. In order that such power should be beyond ordinary reach, the Lord indicated this by announcing the Holy Spirit. They would not rely on their human judgment to remit or retain sins, for the Spirit would enlighten and guide his Church in the exercise of this discretionary power.

But first of all Jesus breathed upon them. He had never previously used this "sign." More explicitly than the imposition of hands, this breathing shows that the power confided to the Church springs from the love of Jesus' heart, wounded by the sins of men. He could institute the Eucharist only on the eve of his death, because this meal is bound up with the sacrifice of his Body and Blood, tortured and spilled for the remission of the sins of men. While assurance of our salvation was linked to his resurrection, it was from the breast of the risen Christ that the breath of the new life to forgive us had to come. The apostles would have plenty of time to ponder the Master's words and appreciate the power with which they had been invested. They already realized that their conception of the messianic kingdom had been finally swept away by the miracle of the Resurrection. It was no longer a question of taking up arms to deliver Israel and to coerce the nations into

W/o pride could there be war?

accepting God's law. They were armed with quite a different force, entirely spiritual, for the purpose of liberating all people from the slavery of sin.

Without losing ourselves in nationalistic dreams as did the Israel of old, still we would gladly assign objective and terrestrial limits to the work of the Redemption. Peace in the world, among peoples and among classes of society, has only one enemy: sin. What are the threats to peace? They are always the same: greed, envy, thirst for power, ambition, and love of money. Sins, and still more sins, are the sources of man's misery. To expect Christianity automatically to establish good governments, just economic laws, and equitable social conditions would be to fall into the old illusion of an earthly kingdom of God.

What Christianity offers to the world is Christ's victory over sin, the remission of sins by his Church, and the gift of a new life which, because it is a life with God, can establish fraternal relations among all.

# THE APOSTLE WHO COULD NOT BELIEVE

*Thomas answered him, "My Lord and my God!"*

–John 20:28

B y Easter Sunday evening, ten apostles and several disciples and women believed that Jesus had risen. Surely this knowledge would have prompted them to hurry back to Galilee in obedience to the angels' message. Yet, according to St. John, eight days afterward the disciples were once more within the Upper Room. So they were still in Jerusalem.

Jerusalem was not safe for the friends of Jesus, and they had to leave as soon as possible. It may be that most of the disciples and the women had returned to Galilee without delay, but their departure does not exclude a decision on the part of the eleven to stay in Jerusalem as discreetly as the situation demanded. We are also confronted with St. Matthew's statement that the eleven disciples journeyed into Galilee, to the mountain where Jesus had told them to meet him. Yet there is no evidence to say when this rendezvous had been fixed by the Savior: whether on the evening of the Resurrection or on the following Sunday. The apostles had good reason for prolonging their stay in Jerusalem before returning to Galilee.

The behavior of the ten on the day after the Resurrection can easily be imagined. They joyfully told the news of the Resurrection to the brethren whom they met in the city. Not everyone was convinced, but the ten would not reproach anyone for disbelieving. Had they not themselves on the previous evening rejected the very idea of any such miracle? The Lord himself had difficulty in allaying their remaining doubts. They merely tried to convince the others.

Now there happened to be one among these others, Thomas, whose Greek name is Didymus, whose prestige strengthened the opposition of those who showed themselves skeptical. Thomas was indeed a serious matter. During the appearance on the evening of Easter Sunday, the apostolic college had received its mission of preaching the good news of salvation in the name of the Messiah, who had entered into his glory. And this first apostolate would naturally be exercised in Galilee, where most of Jesus' disciples were. Thomas' attitude, however, forbade them to begin at once, for it would risk the possibility of dissension. What confusion if one of the apostles denied what the others were asserting! When speaking about St. Thomas we may well call him "the apostle who was unable to believe." It would surely do him an injustice to suggest that he was unwilling to believe. The clearest cases are often also the most complex, and that of Didymus is no exception to the rule. Let us first see what can be said in his defense.

His good will is beyond question. Otherwise, Jesus would not have treated him as condescendingly as he did. Thomas certainly expressed his demands brusquely, but this was due less to pride than to his cast of character. An example occurred some weeks earlier. Other apostles had tried to dissuade Jesus from returning to Bethany, where Lazarus had just died. But

Thomas had not supported their caution. He had not ceased to love the Master, with whom he had been prepared to let himself be stoned. Whence then his obstinate demand to see the Savior, whom the others said they had seen, if not from some unacknowledged jealousy, which in itself is a proof of love? Deep inside, he was suffering from not having seen him, and he ardently desired to do so. Can we be sure that he was not secretly praying, "Master, if you have indeed risen, let me see you!" He wanted to believe, but he could not.

He could not believe, he declared, because he had not seen. Beware of condemning him too quickly for a lack of humility; perhaps for Thomas a higher concern and a sense of loyalty were at stake. When we realize from their first preaching what great importance the apostles attached to their role as official witnesses to the risen Christ, we have to admit that Didymus would have found himself disqualified, perhaps forced to abandon the apostolate, unless he were able to certify personally to the fact on which the Church's teaching relied.

What then were his fellow apostles asking of him? That he should return with them to Galilee to attest that Jesus was alive. How could he testify to what he had not seen? His demand does not seem unreasonable either to the Lord or to the other apostles, from whom he has no wish to separate himself. And therein lies the drama. He wants to remain a member of their company, yet he is unable to accept their assurances. The ten were ultimately to relapse into silence, because their insistence was only hardening his inability to believe. Indeed, they were less scandalized by his obstinacy than concerned about his confusion and suffering. The reason is what Jesus is about to make us understand. Our Lord, in fact, did not show himself to Thomas privately as he had done to Cephas and James. Such a favor would have seemed to approve the apostle's error. On the contrary, Thomas tried to subordinate his faith to a personal experience, and God does not submit to such compulsions. Thomas wanted to establish his conviction by himself, and the Lord left him to himself—that is, to his inability to reach the light unaided. The others quoted to him the passages of Scripture that Jesus had cited to Cleophas. Thomas examined them but could reach no conclusion: Texts were open to so many interpretations. Six days of solitary research only resulted in even greater darkness. Alone he would never be able to believe. For that reason, though not surrendering but perhaps admitting to himself that pride had some part in his denials, he joined his companions, and concealed the doubt that was gnawing at him.

Then, because Thomas was with them, the Lord returned under the same conditions as on the preceding Sunday, with every door closed and with the same greeting of peace. The others had spoken the truth, and in front of them the doubter was going to be confounded and would make honorable amends. Jesus immediately focused in on Thomas: "Put your finger here, and see my hands; and put out your hand, and place it in my side; do not be faithless, but believing" (Jn 20:27). Yes, it was indeed the Lord.

More than by his wounds, Didymus recognized his way of speaking, which was not that of an offended master but of a sympathetic friend. Thomas used the opportunity that Jesus was giving him and seized the Savior's scarred hand, which gave him a certainty that surpassed all the visible proofs. Then grace caused the most splendid faith to burst forth from his long-troubled conscience.

But incidents of this kind could not be tolerated again, nor could private judgment be allowed the right to prevail against that of the Church. So it was to be for the millions of faithful that were to come, who would believe in the Resurrection on the word of witnesses. Jesus did not say that we should be more blessed than the apostles who had seen him, but that we should share their blessedness. Our blessedness would be equal to theirs because our faith would be the same.

If you see + examine the risen Jesus, doesn't that take away faith b/c now you have proof?

# On the Lakeshore

*"Lord, you know everything; you know that I love you."*
*Jesus said to him, "Feed my sheep."*

−John 21:17

The Resurrection, by opening up unexpected horizons for the apostles, set the Master's teaching in its true and complete light. This new preaching during the forty days was as it were a revision of the previous teaching. And what better setting could there have been than Galilee, where they had so often talked together?

The first of these appearances occurred shortly after the apostles had returned to Galilee, when the miraculous catch of fish took place on Lake Tiberias. St. John's account is that of a witness; it is taken straight from life. After the eleven returned from Jerusalem, they went their separate ways home to their own families, but several who lived near the lake met one another and quite naturally resumed their former occupation, fishing. And as they were so working, Jesus appeared to them a third time after his resurrection. What memories this lake held of the unforgettable beginnings of their great adventure! Jesus preaching from Simon's boat, the crowds on the shore listening for hours on end, but above all, that afternoon when they had moved out far from land and their two boats had almost sunk beneath the weight of the huge catch of fish. On that occasion, Simon, Andrew, and the two sons of Zebedee left their nets to follow Jesus and became fishers of men.

As they were returning to the shore with the first light of day, when they were still a hundred yards or more from the shore, they heard someone calling. On the shore, an unknown figure was pointing out to them a shoal of fish on their right; they had not noticed it from the boats. No sooner had they cast the net than it filled up so much that they could scarcely hold it. Instantly they identified the person standing on the shore. John was the first to call out, "It is the Lord!" On hearing that, Simon Peter left his companions holding the net and jumped into the water to get to the shore as quickly as he could, before any of the others. They too moved swiftly, pulling on the oars and dragging the loaded net behind the boat. The sight they beheld when they reached the shore left them speechless. Jesus had lit a fire with his own hands and had started to cook some bread and fish: Jesus, who had not come to be served but to serve. Now how could they doubt that he was really alive, he whom they knew well and now recognized?

With all the assurance of old, the Master paid attention to every detail: "Bring some of the fish that you have just caught" (Jn 21:10). Quickly Peter leaped toward the boat and directed the landing of the catch. The anglers threw the small fry back into the lake and kept only the best fish, which they laid out on the beach, counting them as they did so: one hundred and fifty-three of them. Ancient students of exegesis went to great pains to discover the symbolism of this number. Of all the interpretations, not the least ingenious is that which, noting that one hundred and fifty-three kinds of fish were known to antiquity, suggested that the miraculous catch was an image of the universality of the Redemption.

When Jesus had predicted Peter's denial, had he not added that Peter would nevertheless one day return to him to be the support of his brethren? He renewed his declaration now in front of John, James, Nathaniel, and Thomas, who wanted proof of everything. He deliberately preferred not to have all the eleven present, as that would have made it seem like a re-investiture or public rehabilitation. Nothing which had preceded his death had been changed; on the contrary, everything he had foretold was about to be accomplished. His Church was just entering history, and Peter was to be its head. Not that any of the disciples would have dared dispute the prerogatives formerly granted to Peter; but the Lord wished to restore his apostle's confidence. So before the triple renewal of his mandate, he would three times give him the opportunity of boldly proclaiming his loyalty. Three times: the only allusion to be made to his three denials.

When they had eaten, Jesus said to Simon Peter: Simon, son of John (he does not call him Cephas as this name might revive his remorse), do you love me more than these others? It is a direct question, and causes the apostle some concern. Was he to reply in front of them all, in front of John, that his devotion to the Master was greater than theirs? Only a short while ago he had boasted about it, before he betrayed Jesus. He was uneasy. Jesus had specifically said "more than these." His intention is obvious, for Peter, called to be the first among them, would have to do greater and better service—that is, to love more than they.

Peter would let the Lord judge his boundless affection. He replied humbly, "Yes, Lord; you know that I love you."

Simon was not rash and the Master appreciated his reserve, for in asking him a second time, he made no further reference to the others. He asked simply, "Do you love me?" But why this repetition? No doubt it was pleasing to the Lord to receive a fresh assurance of his devotion, and pleasing to Peter to give it again. But at the third time the disciple's eyes, which had wept so often, could scarcely restrain the tears: Peter was deeply moved when he was asked a third time "Do you love me?" Did Jesus not trust him? Was Peter indignant or despairing? Rather, he abandoned himself to the Lord. Sadness made his voice more loving: "Lord, you know everything; you know that I love you." Jesus said to him, "Feed my sheep" (see John 21:15-17). We may notice here that if Jesus did not remind Peter of his past sins, neither did he ask him to promise any undertaking for the future. Our Lord does not ask us about the future; he asks us to hold firmly to the present: "Simon, son of John, do you love me?" Everything is contained in that. Your present love, Jesus implies, shows me your real sorrow for the past; it shows me that you have a humbler and more prudent will for the future. Every one of us must learn from Jesus how to forgive those who have trespassed against us: without demanding explanations, without imposing conditions, without reserve. And from Peter we must learn the love by which a sinner ought to respond to God's forgiveness.

Our Lord only asks that our love be sufficient to repent with humility and generosity, yet with complete abandonment to his grace. He asks us this single question: "Do you love me?" So often we have replied, "Lord, you know that I love you," and soon afterward we have betrayed him. Were we not sincere when we promised not to offend him anymore? With our hand on our heart, we were firmly resolved to remain loyal to him.

But he who knows all things knew both that we loved him and that we should again be unfaithful to him. When shall we be convinced that it is not our love but his that will save us?

# On the Mountain

*"Go therefore and make disciples of all nations,*
*baptizing them in the name of the Father and of the Son*
*and of the Holy Spirit."*

–Matthew 28:19

The redemption of the world won and merited by Jesus Christ alone will be put into effect by his Church. This fact was among the instructions that the risen Lord wished to recall to his disciples. He did this especially when he appeared to them on a mountain in Galilee.

This appearance differs in one respect from those which preceded it. Whereas formerly he had shown himself without warning, this latest appearance was, so to speak, by appointment. "Now the eleven disciples went to Galilee, to the mountain to which Jesus had directed them. And when they saw him they worshiped him; but some doubted" (Mt 28:16–17).

Was this meeting attended by other disciples as well as by the eleven? Some writers think so, on the grounds that St. Paul, writing in the year 52, says "he appeared to more than five hundred brethren at one time, most of whom are still alive" (1 Cor 15:6). In view of the number of witnesses, it would be most surprising if such an important event were not to be mentioned in the Gospels. A gathering of this magnitude was inconceivable in Jerusalem, near the Sanhedrin and the Praetorium; it must have taken place in Galilee. Earlier, at the Sermon on the Mount, where there were many listeners, Jesus had addressed himself primarily to the disciples standing near him. Was it not likewise in Galilee? Only the eleven were mentioned because they were the leaders, while several hundred disciples may have been ranged behind them.

In any case, the Lord was in fact going to preach a second Sermon on the Mount. The first had outlined the whole gospel program; the second was to provide for its dissemination throughout the world. To these men whom he was sending forth to conquer the entire world for him, the Lord affirmed his own omnipotence. Their Christ had overcome the world; it belonged to him by right, and it was now their task, the Church's task, to transform that right into a fact. "Go forth," he said to them. Their mission, a prolongation of his own, flowed from his sovereignty and his power; it was as a conqueror that he was sending them forth to take possession of the world. Isaiah had prophesied that all the Gentiles on earth would be converted to the true God. The Savior repeated and confirmed this prophecy: "Teach all nations." Their weapons were those which Jesus had used. He sent them out without gold, silver, scholarly diplomas, or any of those things which give men influence and prestige. Their credentials were to be the miracles that God would perform through them. But the gospel contains the power to convince. They must preach the good news everywhere, with its doctrine of salvation.

That the gospel should be proclaimed to all peoples came as no surprise to them, for the prophets had said clearly enough that all nations would be converted to the God of Israel. But the means that Jesus was leaving them for carrying out the religious conquest of the whole world were very different from what they had expected.

Although Jesus instructed them to preach only to the Chosen People, very few had been converted. Now were they to convert not only their fellow countrymen but all the inhabitants of the earth, whose languages they could not even speak? These countless peoples were to be made disciples of Jesus! The apostles were to preach humility and gentleness to the Romans, who were intoxicated with power and whose legions made the earth tremble; they must preach the glorious folly of the Cross to the argumentative Greeks. They were to talk of brotherly love to communities where slavery was rife, and of the heavenly Father to those who worshipped deities dedicated to every vice.

One point however remained obscure in this future pregnant with conquest and suffering: Would there be sufficient time to preach the gospel to all before the world disappeared? Would all be present when Christ returned at the end of time? Or would there be others to take up their work? It is remarkable how after the wonders of Pentecost, the primitive Church organized its evangelistic work slowly, never thinking of hurrying to the four corners of the earth. Ten years later, not one pagan had yet been baptized.

The Lord demands from us also the same zeal and the same patience in fulfilling the mission that his Church will never complete. Until the last day the faithful will have to repeat the prayer he taught them, without any modification: "Thy kingdom come." Truth be told, the work of evangelization begins afresh with every new generation, for adherence to the gospel is a strictly personal, individual step.

*Part Two*

# THE LITURGY
# FROM EASTER
# TO PENTECOST

# Easter Season

*If then you have been raised with Christ, seek the things*
*that are above, where Christ is, seated at the right hand*
*of God. Set your minds on things that are above, not on*
*things that are on earth.*

−Colossians 3:1−2

D uring Easter week we read a complete account of the appearances of the risen Savior and and once again consider the proofs on which our faith rests. All our dogmas would be mere hypotheses and our hopes mere illusions if we were not certain of the fact that Jesus Christ rose from the dead. Having established this fact, the liturgy goes on to tell us that we must now *live* by this belief.

Eastertime was first called *Pentekoste,* a period of fifty days. Easter and Pentecost were two terms used for a single feast. At Easter the victory of Jesus Christ freed humanity from sin and loosed it from death. But when he emerged from the sepulchre the Lord did not come back to share his apostles' existence; he returned to his Father in heaven where that divine life which exists on earth only as it were in seed, flourishes to the full. That divine seed, which on earth transforms our condition and assures our future destiny, was bestowed on us by Jesus after his ascent to heaven, when he sent the Holy Spirit to take possession of his Church. That was on the fiftieth day after his resurrection. Easter, the Ascension, and Pentecost are in fact three aspects of the same saving mystery, which forms a single whole. That is why the three events were originally commemorated together in one festival of fifty days, the feast of feasts.

In the Latin Church, Eastertide lasts for fifty-six days. Although the feasts of Ascension and Pentecost each have their own purpose, the atmosphere of the *Pentekoste* has continued as a time for thanksgiving to Christ for having raised us with him and for resolving to live in the new life which he has communicated to us.

The predominant theme of the Masses in this season is unquestionably one of joy. Our joy during this period must not only consist in exterior manifestations but must reflect our interior determination to lead a life worthy of our triumphal Savior. Those who are baptized are "risen from the dead." They share in the life of the glorified Christ, but this new life is not yet manifest. That divine life remains hidden with Christ in God, but our possession of it is nonetheless real. Therefore, we have not the right to entangle ourselves with this world's goods; we must seek heavenly joys. They are ours because we have risen with Christ.

Faithfulness, rather than the spiritual struggle, is the current theme: Let us become aware of the nobility of our new life, and the sense of our great dignity will lead us away from earthly attractions to concentrate our energies on heavenly things. Here we need asceticism again, to watch ourselves, to avoid all the negligence and cowardice that would hinder this heavenly impetus.

The spirituality is infused throughout with the spirit of the Beatitudes. These formulae, apparently paradoxical inasmuch as they ally happiness with renunciation, promise us the possession of God in one form or another. But the Easter victory has brought the fulfillment of the Savior's promises nearer, for if we are risen with Christ our life is henceforth hidden with Christ in God.

Because we are thinking of heavenly goods, our desire of holiness compels us to establish justice on earth; we thirst for this and are prepared to face any persecution for it. But our reward is great before God, in whom we are already living, hidden with Jesus Christ.

# RENEWAL

*Like newborn babes, long for the pure spiritual milk, that*

*by it you may grow up to salvation.*

–1 Peter 2:2

First Sunday after Easter: On this first Sunday, the Roman community used to assemble at the church dedicated to St. Pancras, who was martyred at the age of twelve or fourteen. When baptism was administered but once a year (*solennis*), during the nocturnal vigil of Easter, the neophytes, accompanied by their godparents, took part in a Eucharistic celebration every morning throughout the octave, and in the afternoon they attended vespers in one of Rome's great basilicas. Throughout the week they wore white albs, which completely enveloped them. The faithful loved to watch or follow this white procession as it wound its way through the city streets, especially from the fifth century onwards, when the newly baptized included not only adults but also adolescents and children.

But everything has an end, and after vespers on Easter Saturday, the octave day of their baptism, they deposited in the sacristy their white robes, to be used the following year by other candidates. St. Peter compares these newly baptized to newborn infants, free from malice and thirsty for the spiritual milk that will make them grow rapidly. Soon they will mingle with their elders and form with them "a chosen race, a royal priesthood, a holy nation, God's own people" (1 Pt 2:9). Before dismissing them, the pontiff had prayed for them, that they be nourished with the sacrament of redemption, and progress in the true faith. Up to then, they had been prisoners of the world. In a society largely pagan they will still be exposed to the influence of worldly philosophies and allurements, sometimes even to threats. This belief must not be a mere signature penned at the foot of a document. It must be a practical adherence of heart and will to the gift that God placed in their soul when they received the Holy Spirit with the water of baptism and the bread of the Eucharist. For as long as they are in themselves a living testimony of God, nobody and nothing can rob them of their victory.

Yet the enemies of this living faith are not all in the world outside. Those external enemies too often find allies within the believer himself: in his judgment which raises doubts, in his sensitivity which rebels, in his will which so easily tires. Neophytes must beware of setting themselves up as judges of the faith. The Gospel reminds them of the apostle Thomas, to show them the risks they run, left to their own resources. On the other hand, by not separating themselves from the Christian community which they have just entered, by staying close to the Church, they will enjoy sufficient security to safeguard their faith and to live by it.

In order to live by their faith, they have an equally effective means within reach, namely participation in the eucharistic Sacrifice, by which Jesus, the Son of God, is present within the community of Christians, until his visible return to earth. Perseverance applies particularly to us after the penitential exercises of Lent. Each anniversary of the Easter festival that has cleansed us ought to mark a new beginning in our life as baptized Christians; let us not waste the graces it offers us. Let us use them zealously in the daily conduct of our life.

When Christians were baptized, they celebrated both the anniversary of the Lord's resurrection and their own birth into the divine life. Today, the faithful who take part in the ceremonies of Holy Saturday are privileged to relive together the theology and the rites of their baptism. Note how few people think of celebrating the anniversary on which they were baptized. Nothing prevents us from individually making this act of renewal on the octave day of Easter. The Mass text will inspire us and offer us a splendid opportunity.

In order to persevere in the faith, let us try to restore its novelty and freshness by means of a more attentive meditation on the paschal mystery. By Baptism we were made children of God and children of the Church. Let us renew our allegiance to the mystical Body of Christ, that we may thereby become more obedient and more active members. The Church tells us, in one of the proper prayers of the Tridentine Mass,[2] that she is never so jubilant as on this day, so let us not sadden our mother by our indifference; let us not give her cause for anxiety by being isolated from the Church. Let us renew our conviction that we belong to a community which keeps us in line with the true faith. Only the Church can unite us closely to Jesus Christ.

2   This prayer, called the Secret, is the prayer said quietly by the celebrating priest at the end of the Offertory in the Roman Liturgy.

# THE GOOD SHEPHERD

*God of everlasting mercy, who in the very recurrence of the*

*paschal feast, kindle the faith of the people you have made*

*your own…*

−Collect of the Second Sunday of Easter[3]

Second Sunday after Easter (Divine Mercy Sunday): The Good Shepherd image was a familiar one to those listening to Jesus; their ancestors had been shepherds for generations, and its memory had influenced the piety of God's people. Many of the psalms bear traces of it, with phrases such "Shepherd of Israel," "Go out from Egypt like sheep," "The Lord is my Shepherd," "Thy rod and staff shall comfort me." God himself had appropriated this simile and this role when he warned Ezekiel that because of the indifference and perversity of the religious leaders of his people he would cast out those bad shepherds and take their place himself. We should not overlook this magnificent passage, which foreshadows the gospel.

3   The image and meaning of the Good Shepherd was emphasized
    in the former readings of the Second Sunday of Easter. With the
    institution of Divine Mercy Sunday in 2000 by Pope St. John Paul II,
    the readings were revised, and none in the revised liturgy specifically
    refer to Divine Mercy, except the passage above. But the Good Shep-
    herd was a distinct example of mercy to generations, so this chapter
    remains appropriate for this book's latest edition.

Later in history, when our Savior walked through the towns and markets of Galilee, he was deeply moved by the spiritual ignorance of the people that came to hear him. They were like sheep without a shepherd, exhausted and downfallen. Then, in the last months of his ministry, returning to the metaphor by which God had described himself through his prophet, a clear allusion to his divinity, Jesus declared: "I am the Good Shepherd." He would not leave his own without food but would liberally provide for them. Whereas a hireling in charge of sheep not his own might flee when a wild beast threatened the flock, he would protect his sheep because they were his own. He would brave the wolf that tried to snatch them away from him, even though it meant allowing his body to be torn to pieces. What other shepherd would be prepared to do as much?

And Jesus has kept his word. Our sinful world deserved that God should turn away from it, but because he saw it in such a pitiful state the Son of God did more than stoop to our distress: He lowered himself even to becoming one of us; that was the only way of raising us up.

But the most wonderful thing of all has yet to be told. Jesus compares the mutual bond between the shepherd and his sheep to his own knowledge of the Father and the knowledge which the Father has of him. Obviously the comparison is a restricted one since we cannot hope to know Jesus as we are known by him. Rather than a simile, this is an analogy based on the reciprocity and love born of our mutual knowledge.

Yet Jesus has to acknowledge that this unity, realized in those who form his Church, has not extended as far as he would wish. "And I have other sheep, that are not of this fold" (Jn 10:16). The sadness underlying these words is counteracted by the Savior's resolve to save those others also, and by the hope that they will hear his voice. Who are these other sheep? Undoubtedly they are all mankind, though Jesus may here have had in mind particularly "the lost sheep of the house of Israel" (Mt 15:24), who are the object of his personal mission: those sons of Abraham who have not yet responded to his call, and sadder still, the many disciples who, having once believed in him, "drew back and no longer went about with him" (Jn 6:66). These people, who turned away from Christ in such large numbers, had been pre-figured in the action of their ancestors who, on returning from exile to discover their land in ruins, dismissed in anger the prophet Zechariah. The sheep, growing tired of their shepherd, had sent him away, after paying him his salary of thirty pieces of silver.

We must also develop our catholic spirit within the Church. Why speak of discipline and obligations when our love for the one Shepherd should suffice to preserve in us the joy of being united and a determination to remain so? Obedience comes naturally when we remember that Jesus is our Shepherd.

# Faithful
# to the Truth

*O God, who dost show to them that are in error the light*

*of thy truth that they may return into the way of salvation*

*grant to all those who profess themselves Christians to*

*reject those things which are contrary to that name, and*

*follow such things as are agreeable to the same.*[4]

–The Collect of the Mass in the Extraordinary Form,
Third Sunday after Easter

Third Sunday of Easter: The doors of the fold in which Christ gathered his sheep are opened today, and the lambs must face the wolves. How could the Church convert the world without ever entering it? Yesterday's unbelievers must henceforth bear witness to their faith, and yesterday's sinners must set an example by their virtue. This mission also devolves upon Christians in every age, and the primary condition for making it most effective is for us to remain faithful to the truth.

---

4   *Deus, qui errantibus, ut in viam possint redire justitiae, veritatis tuae lumen*
    *ostendis, da cunctis qui Christiana professione censentur, et illa respuere quae*
    *huic inimici sunt nomini, et ea quae apta sunt, sectari.*

The neophytes who had just been "illumined" by baptism—as the saying went even in the days of St. Justin—had until recently been wandering in darkness. Some of them had only just abandoned the myths and vices of paganism. Certain others, belonging to families of whom one parent was Christian, had been destined for the catechumenate since infancy, but the necessity for breaking with the lax customs of their contemporaries had made them postpone such a grave step.

Sometimes, even, a Christian mother would advise this postponement, fearing the effects, on violent and sensual temperaments, of the strict obligations imposed by Christ's teaching. These young people had listened to pagan teachers expounding philosophies that were far more tolerant toward human passions than that "folly of the Cross" being taught by the ministers of the new religion. A few lingered in their erroneous ways, although cold reason showed them the futility of the ancient fables and the moral and social dangers of the pagan mysteries. But a secret influence was to prove more effective than reason in ending their procrastinations and enabling them to seize the "light of truth" which God hides from no one and which never fails to convince men of good will.

However, while these catechumens had rallied to the truth on Easter night, some former baptized persons had returned to the way of truth two days earlier. Those in error, to whom the Collect refers, also included the Christians who had been unfaithful to their baptism. Victims of passions inadequately overcome or of pagan surroundings that had not lost their attraction, they had fallen back into those evil practices which they had promised to renounce. Some had killed an enemy in a fit of anger. Others, for reasons of human respect or to advance their careers, or, in the case of merchants, for fear of losing a rich customer, had taken part publicly in idolatrous rites. Some had been unable to resist the frenzy of mortal struggles in the amphitheater; others had scandalized their companions by their misconduct.

Now the Church could never have succeeded in transforming the customs of the faithful if she had tolerated such lapses into grave sin. Her goodness required her to act mercilessly, so she excluded the guilty from celebrations of the Eucharist, barely suffering them to be present at the beginning of liturgical functions and then only at a considerable distance from the altar. This usually lasted for quite a long period. It was only after they had given unmistakable signs of repentance and proofs of amendment that the bishop would decide to readmit them into the normal life of the Church. These penitents were subjected to a final testing which coincided with Lent; this began for them with the imposition of ashes, and besides fasting they were also required either to wear a hair shirt or to do some other form of penance. The ceremony of reconciliation took place on the morning of Holy Thursday. After being readmitted to the Christian community, they were allowed to take part that same evening in the reunion commemorating the Last Supper. Thus the Church included in her Easter rejoicings the return to the fold of those who had strayed, those to whom God had shown the seriousness of their faults so that they might return into the way of righteousness.

Nevertheless the institution of Lent was not intended solely for catechumens and penitents. The Church has imposed this season of penitence and earnest prayer even on her most faithful children, as a means of reactivating their faith, reinforcing their character, stimulating their conscience—in a word, advancing the ever-incomplete work of their sanctification. Whatever may have been the historical origin of the text we are considering, its implication affects us all in the present. Lent and the liturgy of the great Triduum have brought us new graces of conversion. Before the cross of Calvary we have been able at least to reproach ourselves for our shortcomings and failures, and perhaps correct deviations which were causing us to slip into lukewarmness and mediocrity; and on Easter morning, in the light of the Resurrection, we have rejoined the road of stricter and more fervent loyalty to the teaching and example of our Savior. It is indeed a narrow road, but one along which we travel more easily because we have again found peace in the possession of truth.

Three weeks have passed since Easter; we must not stop, nor retrace our steps along the road. The liturgy of Eastertime seems to have regulated our progress in the new life. First it brought together the people of God, that is, all those who believe that Jesus is the Son of God (First Sunday) and who are loyal to the Church in which Christ has gathered them (Second Sunday). But the Christian community restricts individualism only in order to develop individuality; in consequence the liturgical texts are hereafter addressed to each one's conscience. We do not always have either the leisure or the capacity to consider the implications and results of a decision that has to be taken, sometimes immediately; we need a yardstick by which our conscience can instantly recognize what it ought to reject and what it ought to accomplish. This standard is the very name given to those who profess faith in the Resurrection.

What a beautiful name it is! The Lord's first disciples would never have thought of applying it to themselves; as for the Jews, they would have taken care not to blaspheme the name of the messiah when they were speaking of that sect of Galilean apostates. It was the pagans of Antioch who classed under that name the great number of their compatriots who had been converted to the new faith (Acts 11:26). All these converts were the "people of Christ," the "Christians," who had the one word, *Christos*, on their lips—the name of the crucified man whom they said was alive, whom they worshipped as their God, and for whom they had radically altered their mode of life. A casual nickname has become our title to glory, but it would be usurped if we were not really Christ's, for we claim him as our Master because his teaching is our way of life. How can we proclaim that Christ lives in us if our conduct is contrary to his gospel?

It is only too easy for nonbelievers to criticize us in the ordinary way, but who can refute their criticism when they denounce the absurdity of the unfaithful Christian! "And he dares to call himself a Christian!" Our judgment of ourselves should be no less severe. I am not here referring to those positive evils which are obviously forbidden to all, but to petty failings—acts of selfishness and meanness, cowardice disguised as prudence, acts of spite committed in the name of virtue—and many other similar offenses which make a mockery of our name as Christians. God wants us to reject them with scorn, but that is not sufficient. Our status as Christians requires dignity of life, simplicity in the giving of self, joyful courage in the cause of justice, and tenacity of effort; in short, an unquenchable desire to honor him whose name we bear. What would he think in my place; what would he say and do? Our pride in bearing his name will dictate our course of action and make us live in the truth.

At the present time many people are turned from the teaching of the Christian religion because they fail to see Christians observing its precepts. Metaphysical problems worry comparatively few people. Most men are more concerned with concrete economic problems. Can Christ save them from all these anxieties? Unless we make it our business to try to resolve such problems, we are not being entirely faithful to our name as Christians, and we should be betraying this title if, through fear, we deferred finding a solution. We are right to condemn the solutions of materialistic reformers, but only if we establish a more perfect social order than the one they suggest. Those of our fellow men who are in error will begin to be interested in the truth of Christianity when they can see Christians working, making sacrifices, struggling and suffering with them, in the relief of distress.

Others have abandoned religion for intellectual reasons, but shall we convert them by clever arguments? We may not always have the ability to do this, and in any case controversy rarely persuades anybody. Example is what convinces. Do unbelievers really know what faith is? They imagine it as adherence to a string of dogmatic propositions, when in fact it is primarily attachment to a Person who absorbs us completely. The light we can offer them is the example of a living faith, Christians conquering by Christ, living by his spirit and overflowing with his love.

And then there are many "in error," who are neither unfortunates nor intellectuals. Indifferent rather than unbelieving, they wander through life without asking themselves any questions. They too, if they are to discover the light of truth, need the irreproachable example of our life as Christians. They do not realize that others, the same as themselves and in similar circumstances of life, are preparing themselves for a supernatural destiny. No words of ours can convince them of this reality, but if we live side by side with them as true Christians, humble and unselfish, detached from love of money, content with our lot, trusting in God despite tomorrow's uncertainties, strong in suffering and smiling in adversity, then they will know that there really are some for whom heaven is not just a myth.

# ALIENS AND EXILES

*I beseech you as aliens and exiles.… Maintain good*
*conduct among the Gentiles.*

−1 Peter 2:11–12

*A*liens and exiles was an Old Testament concept used to
describe our earthly life. St. Peter applied it for the
Christians of his time as a standard of conduct for a
minority group in a pagan society. In order to better understand
his warnings, as well as the idea behind the whole letter, we
need to recall in what circumstances he was writing in Rome
to the Christian communities scattered all over Asia Minor.

The letter was written shortly before Nero's persecutions,
almost certainly in the year 63. St. Peter was well-placed for
observing the first rumblings of the approaching storm, for
the wind had turned against the newly born Church, which
up to then had flourished remarkably. Its freedom rested on
the privilege of retaining their national religion that was
enjoyed by the Jewish colonies scattered throughout the
Roman empire. In the eyes of the authorities, Christianity
itself had at first passed for a Jewish sect. However, in the
year 49, during the reign of Claudius, a decree banished from
Rome those Jews who were guilty of "having stirred up
trouble in that city, *impulsore Chresto*," as Suetonius wrote, "at

the instance of a certain Christ," whom the historian clearly took to be an agitator.

The Jews began to reject the renegades in their midst, in order to be disassociated from them in the eyes of the government and popular opinion, and the breach between the synagogue and the Church was effected almost everywhere. Christianity consequently became an autonomous religious society that could no longer claim the tolerance accorded to Judaism. The Christians came once more under the ordinary laws and so were compelled to observe the state religion, and particularly the worship of the god-emperor. Since they refused to do so, the pagans considered them impious people against whom Nero, having set fire to the city, tried to stir up popular indignation.

St. Peter's epistle should be read against this background. The Christians were hated by the pagans. Should they then withdraw among themselves and establish ghettos, thus responding to hatred by a show of timidity and offended pride? The leader of the Church had no such thought in mind, nor did he wish to suggest any such thing when he reminded them that they were strangers and exiles. The ban imposed on Christians related to the occasions of sin which *were only too numerous among the pagans around them. No compromise would be tolerated in this* respect, or they would be guilty of denying their faith.

But the apostles did not therefore conclude that they should hide or isolate themselves from their neighbors, withdrawing from public life. Far from it: They were to take their place among their fellows. Their life among the Gentiles must be beyond reproach, so that every suspicion about them might be removed. They were obliged to love their brethren, but to remember that their enemies also were entitled to consideration.

They were to be loyal and irreproachable citizens, but obey God first; fear God and honor the sovereign. A thoughtful observer could not begrudge his admiration for that former Galilean fisherman, lost amid the most obscure inhabitants of Rome, as he ordered all his brethren in Christ to honor the man who tomorrow would be their executioner. There is to be neither flattery nor defiance. He proclaims the right and prescribes the duty. The rest is God's affair.

*Aliens and exiles.* Let us observe the meaning of these terms instead of making use of them to camouflage our timidity, or as pretexts for deserting the duties we owe to God and man. St. Peter wishes Christians to bear witness openly, showing themselves as they are without drifting into dangerous opportunism. They need not apologize for being Christians, nor make excuses for being in the limelight. If our behavior were to depend on the strength of our numbers in society or if— sometimes brave, sometimes cowardly—we should present the truth under different banners, then it would no longer be the truth. At all times our conduct must be the same: uniformly upright and inspired by our faith. With regard to the principles which the apostle lays down concerning civil action, these clearly show that the teaching of the Church was thoroughly defined from the first years of its existence. For those who read it attentively, this Epistle of St. Peter expresses above all the concept that the Christian is a free man; he is the freest of all citizens. This concept was expressed at a time when slaves abounded and when citizens were the concern of the state. The freedom of others is as sacred to the Christian as his own personal freedom. Although Peter plainly professes respect for the emperor when exercising his legitimate functions, he denies him the right to interfere with faith. The apostle remains faithful to God, and allows himself to be crucified upside down without speaking ill of the sovereign. The Christian's freedom of action is equally bound by the divine laws. These constitute both the limits of his obedience to men and the limits of his own independence. His profound respect for freedom prevents him from taking unfair advantage of it; he knows that he must not resort to unworthy means to serve the purposes of good. The twin beacons of honesty and unselfishness mark his course.

# YET A LITTLE WHILE

*"[Y]ou will weep and lament, but the world will rejoice;*
*you will be sorrowful, but your sorrow will turn into joy."*

–John 16:20

We acclaim the risen Christ yet bear in mind that he entered his glory only through suffering. The Christian must not hope for a different fate. His joy is not the product of his imagination, nor a flight into unreality; for him also it is the fruit of the Cross. The Epistle of St. Peter has already shown us the Church facing heathen opposition. Our Lord hastens to add that our present afflictions need not discourage us, for our sadness will be of short duration and will be changed to joy.

The unhappy men were overwhelmed with grief, and their Master wished to comfort them. Yet he tells them two things that they fail to understand; first, his departure to the Father, then his return to them. We in our turn ask what this brief delay may signify, for our Lord's reply is open to two interpretations. At first sight Jesus would seem to be alluding to the Resurrection which was to follow his death. Yet a little while—some hours, the last hours of their intimacy—and the apostles would not see him. Their hearts would be embittered, while their enemies would rejoice.

But the separation would be a short one. Yet a little while, at least three days, and they would see him again, and their sorrow would be turned to joy.

Yet this explanation of the "little while" is not entirely satisfactory. Would not Jesus first of all have to "go to the Father"? Yet he only returned thence on Ascension Day. Moreover, the context of the farewell discourse is most explicit about the nature of the trials which were in store for the apostles, while the world would rejoice—the world at large and not merely the Jews who were responsible for the death of Jesus. The Lord did not hide from them the persecutions that the world reserved for them. These predictions undoubtedly refer to a time after the Resurrection, and are concerned with the fate of the apostles after Jesus had returned to the Father.

St. Augustine favored this opinion. Commenting on the Latin text, which is made even more obscure by the final remark, "because I go to the Father," he advised transposing it to read thus: "Yet a little while and you will not see me, because I go to my Father; yet a little while and you will see me again." Jesus would then have had in view his return at the end of time, the everlasting joy of the Church when the Parousia arrives, which was inaugurated on the morning of the Resurrection, and for each of his disciples there was heaven waiting after earth's struggles. The parable of the woman in childbirth removes any remaining doubts as to the Savior's real meaning. A young mother, after the great pain of labor, forgets her sufferings for joy that a child is born into the world. So the Church, harassed by the attacks of her enemies and sworn to remain faithful to her Head through renunciations and sacrifices, will when Jesus returns no longer remember her sufferings on earth, so great will be her joy at having given birth to a new humanity, a divine race.

This joy which our Lord promises to his disciples nothing can take from them. This primary truth of Christianity—that the sufferings of the apostles will make their mission more effective, just as the grain of wheat only produces other ears when it dies in the soil—can easily be deduced from this passage in the Gospel, although it does not appear as direct teaching.

Our Lord is warning us that by being his disciples we shall of necessity suffer persecution. It is something that is for our good, and to it we shall be indebted for a joy out of all proportion to the pain we have endured. It is a blessing for us, a personal blessing, apart altogether from any consideration of the fruitfulness of our apostolate and the conversion of the world, which are other causes for joy.

It is this personal benefit from persecution that Jesus emphasizes. It was necessary that Christ should suffer on behalf of men in order to enter into his glory; it is equally necessary that Christians should be oppressed in this world in order to enter into the glory of their Lord. Our redemption was effected by Jesus and can only be through him; it was not effected for all at one time, but it is effected for each individual in the course of our life. We shall have a share in our Savior's redemption on condition that we pass, as he did, from defeat to victory, from the cross to glory.

Confidence is not inactivity. We do not become converted in order to fall asleep in a false security. We are saved indeed. We have not yet arrived; we are still on our way, the way of the cross. Though Jesus has guaranteed to his Church that the powers of darkness will not prevail against her, that is no reason for taking refuge in passive neutrality. On the contrary, what else does it mean but that the forces of evil will battle relentlessly against the Church and that she must resist them without ceasing? And we are the Church, aren't we?

Consider which periods in her history have most clearly revealed her sanctity and her vitality. It was not during the time when Caesar was loading her with favors, but when he was disputing her rights over men's consciences; not when she was enjoying the world's honors and riches, but when she was being subjected to harassments and plundering. "The faith only flourishes," wrote Frederick Ozanam, the founder of the St. Vincent de Paul Society, "where it is faced with a government that is either alien or hostile. That does not mean we must ask God to give us bad governments: but we must not keep looking for a government that will do our work for us and assume a task regarding our fellow-men which God never entrusted to it. We must forge ahead and extend our personal influence among men."[5]

During those periods when it is not easy for us to be Christians because the world is attacking the Church, persecution unfortunately causes some apostasy. On the other hand, such times also produce sterling generosity and heroic fidelity. The Church is indeed grieved to see bloodshed, and she prays ceaselessly that God will grant the peace that is necessary for her work. But do not imagine that she comes to terms with the enemy, for that would not be peace but betrayal. Though persecutions occurring from time to time are part of God's plan to lead the Church to her essential purity, the individual Christian must always endure the criticism, animosity, and hostility of the world.

Whatever may be the lifespan of the Church and of the world, the time of preparation for the immeasurable bliss to

5  *Letters*, Book 2, p. 312.

come is bound by the limits of an earthly life, and is therefore of short duration. This was true for the apostles to whom Jesus was speaking, and it is true for each one of us. Only a little while is left in which to suffer, yet it is long enough for us to increase our love.

# A PRAYER FOR CONSTANCY

*Almighty ever-living God, lead us to a share in the joys of heaven, so that the humble flock may reach where the brave Shepherd has gone before.*

—Collect for the Fourth Sunday after Easter

ourth Sunday after Easter: Jesus is about to rejoin his Father, where we can pray to him and from where he will send the Holy Spirit to bear witness to his work and continue it; where also on the day of general resurrection he will reveal himself to all who have loved him. Our Savior goes before us to heaven where a place is being prepared for us. We must dwell there in spirit now, we must fix our minds on it. What is the Christian's goal if not that happiness which will completely satisfy all aspirations and longings?

When fate smiles on us, our duties seem light, and, in the absence of major crises, we may mistake our good practices for virtue. Virtue, however, only comes through effort and struggle. The facile virtue we boast of is rudely shaken when adversity intervenes, but, in God's plan, it is adversity which compels us to progress. The value of our lives depends on what we do with our joys and sorrows. It is true that we rarely choose the conditions of our existence, whether they be health or sickness, riches or poverty, honors or humiliations. Moreover, our conditions of life are ceaselessly being modified; we pass swiftly from laughter to tears and we soon change from grief to joy. But since all around us is transient, we must look higher than the earth and fix our hearts upon God, who orders all things. Then events will not deflect us from our course; it is we who will dominate the events. We shall use them to acquire real virtues.

The law of Christ bids us to "fix our hearts," to lead only one life, the life that God has allotted us in his plan. There, only, are true joys to be found, in the secret of our own trade or in the exercise of our family duties. When we feel helpless, we have only to implore God for the necessary constancy to remain faithful to the truth. Only God can in fact communicate something of his immutability to us; and it is prayer that has given us the certainty of this power. Its action is sufficient to bring about the unification of our will.

The primitive community in Jerusalem had at once realized this unity: "Now the company of those who believed were of one heart and soul" (Acts 4:32). God creates among his faithful people the unanimous desire to conform to his plan, but by the very fact that the will of all is identical, the will of each one is unchangeable. And there we have a solemn guarantee against the reverses which circumstances can inflict on us, against deviations of our personal judgment, and against the world's perversions.

In order to resist the attraction of all other pleasures, it is important that God's will should be pleasing to us, and that, before every other consideration, we should follow the spontaneous reflex that flows from a heart already aflame with the love of God.

# JESUS AND THE
# WORLD ON TRIAL

*"And when he comes, he will convince the world of sin*

*and of righteousness and of judgment."*

–John 16:8

On the night of Holy Thursday our Lord tried to alleviate the sorrow of his apostles. It was true that he was going to leave them, but wasn't it for their benefit that he was going away? He could not send them the Holy Spirit until after he had returned to the Father. Yet the disciples' sadness served as a trial for their faith. In their despair at seeing the Master condemned, would they not conclude that his mission was a failure? So Jesus must encourage them now and sustain their hearts.

A monstrous trial was about to take place in the holy city. The world was going to put on trial, and to condemn, the Son of God. The world, in the moral sense, represents all sinners in revolt against God. But in St. John's writings, and particularly here, the world is more precisely represented by the authorities and the elite, the blind and apostate leaders of the people.

When Jesus was speaking to his disciples, the world was about to triumph, a temporary and essentially superficial triumph. The Lord's judges were going to accuse him of having sinned. Charging him with blasphemy, they set themselves up as the defenders of divine justice; they would condemn him to death. In order to help his disciples endure this ignominious travesty of justice, the Master warned them that the Comforter whom he would send them would quickly reestablish the truth.

The Holy Spirit was coming to rehabilitate our Lord and to reverse the odious trial he was to endure. This reversal would fall under three occurences.

First, the Spirit will address the lack of belief. The Paraclete will throw back on the accusers the charge which they had preferred against Jesus—they will be universally recognized as being solely to blame. As soon as the Holy Spirit comes and the apostles begin to preach the gospel, the wrongfulness of the leaders will be made clear and their age-old prerogatives will be taken away from them. The Lord of the vineyard will lease his vineyard to other workers.

Second, the counsel for the defense will likewise reveal, when he comes to earth, that Jesus is indeed holy, and much more, that he is the Holy One of God. His resurrection will be the proof of his divinity. It is true that only a small number of witnesses, chosen in advance, will see the risen Savior, but all will know that he has returned in his divine glory; since not until after he has returned to heaven will the Lord send his Spirit to take possession of the Church. So the Paraclete will bear witness that Jesus is sitting at the right hand of the Father, that he is God, and that he is the Son of God.

Third, the Spirit will show the world and Satan, its leader, that they have indeed been mistaken in condemning the Savior. Satan thought he had triumphed on Good Friday, but it was he who was overcome on that day, when sinful man was redeemed. By sending Jesus to his death, he little suspected that he was going to lose the prey that had been his since Adam's fall, nor that he was contributing to our salvation.

# THE LAW OF FREEDOM

*But he who looks into the perfect law, the law of liberty,*
*and perseveres, being no hearer that forgets but a doer that*
*acts, he shall be blessed in his doing.*

–James 1:25

Fifth Sunday after Easter: We have good reason to thank God for having delivered his people. but are we really free of what impedes us from following Jesus Christ? If we have merely listened to our Savior's message of liberation and have not behaved like free people, then we are deluding ourselves. The Christian would also be quite mistaken to count on his own unaided efforts in imitating the holiness of Jesus.

Jesus knows his true disciples by the way they act upon his words, as he himself says in the Sermon on the Mount (Lk 6:46). In several places the Epistle of St. James is a commentary on that sermon. That need not surprise us, as James the Less was a near relation of our Savior. A son of the Blessed Virgin's sister, it is generally believed that he lived in more intimate contact with Jesus, and for a longer time, than did the other apostles. This doubtless explains why our Lord appeared to him after the Resurrection. Furthermore, he has in common with his Master the same imagery of style, as will be seen from the parable of the man who beholds himself in a mirror.

A man, while dressing, looks at himself in the mirror, and even looks attentively. Perhaps he notices that his hair is untidy, or he may even detect a blemish on his face. But he has other things to think about, possibly his business or an urgent appointment—in short he forgets the flaws that the mirror reveals to him. His wife reproaches him for being either absent-minded or incurably careless. Such, according to the apostle, is the illogical position of the Christian who hears the Word of God but does not permit it to influence his life. The epistle then proceeds to illustrate the other type of disciple, who gazes attentively on the law of Christ and prolongs his contemplation of it. The mirror of perfection, which is the gospel, reveals to him the points which need attending to in his moral countenance, the inherent weaknesses of temperament and character. Unlike the first man, shallow and negligent, who did not attend to his faults and continued to be self-satisfied, the second man does not forget the personal message which the Lord has addressed to him.

The gospel as the mirror of our lives! That is an ingenious idea, for we can learn a lesson from it that is often misunderstood. Many Christians, keen to make spiritual progress, mark time and become discouraged because of the incorrect use they make of their examination of conscience. They reduce this indispensable exercise to a long and scrupulous review of their everyday faults. They become weighed down by these and look only at them, or else they weary of seeing nothing but their own moral poverty. Or if they occasionally overcome some fault, they tend to be satisfied with what is, in reality, just honest mediocrity.

St. James leaves his readers to work out for themselves the applications of his simile of the Christian in front of the mirror. By way of example he selects one of those negligent hearers who forget the word as soon as they have heard it. That man, he says, believes he is religious because he attends to his religious duties, yet he cannot curb his tongue. He may be boastful, indiscreet, a slanderer, or use coarse words in his speech, but he still pays no heed to what he has read in the Gospels. If our piety is not accompanied by irreproachable moral behavior and active charity, then we are not in any way religious or Christian. Either we have not read the Gospels at all or else we have forgotten their message. On the other hand, he whose behavior is beyond reproach and who unselfishly devotes himself to others is the *factor verbi*. The meditated word influences his actions.

# ON THE WAY
# TO THE FATHER

*"I came from the Father and have come into the world;*

*again, I am leaving the world and going to the Father."*

–John 16:28

ifth Sunday after Easter: The feast of the Ascension recalls our Lord's last appearance to his disciples before returning to his place at the Father's right hand. He will not visibly appear again in this world until he returns to end its course, his human mission completed. The *Father* and the *world* are the two poles of our Lord's two-way journey. The Creator and his creation: This is the deepest and sweetest of mysteries—the love of the infinite Being for those not yet in existence. What prompted God to call into existence the innumerable worlds which make up the universe, and in the immensity of this system to create a very tiny planet, our earth, and fill it with myriads of living things who are completely ignorant of the reason for their existence and incapable even of putting the question to themselves?

*God is love.* This fact and no other explains the strange mystery, and illuminates the darkness of man's mind. Love needs to expand, to give itself and prove itself. Love wants to create happy people; God called us into being with the object of sharing his own happiness. It is for this that his infinite power has caused this wealth of planets and profusion of life to spring forth out of nothing. The world does not only have a Creator, it also has a Father.

We showed ourselves incapable of achieving either our noblest ambitions or the will of God. We were foundering in waywardness and sin. God saw the futile sterility of our efforts but did not abandon us to our own nothingness. Instead, one of the Divine Persons, yielding to an even more prodigious love than creation love, "made himself nothing," as it were, in order to come among us and take his place in our human race. The Father accepted the offering of his beloved Son and proved his acceptance by delivering Jesus from the bonds of death. Henceforth man, now reconciled to God, will live the very life of the risen Christ. Our Lord is now able to withdraw, his mission completed.

We owe our life to him. He put us into the world to fulfill the task he has appointed us to do, and, in his plan, we only leave the world to go to him. God is our beginning and our end, our master and inspirer, the objective of our life. We came from God and we are going back to God—that is the itinerary of all human life. What then is the life of the Christian? Our function on earth consists in re-enacting the mission for which the Son of God came into the world: to serve the Father in every sphere of our activity. We must behave as sons and daughters, obedient to all our Father's wishes, following the example of Christ. We must show the Father to others by our charity toward them. In this way we contribute to the salvation of the whole human family. Our work is the work of Christ himself. Reverses, injustices, contradictions, bitterness, and sufferings are all part of the lot of Christians who are on their way to the Father, for we shall be leaving the world to go to the Father.

# CHRIST OUR
# ADVOCATE IN HEAVEN

*While he blessed them, he parted from them*
*and was carried up into heaven. And they worshiped him,*
*and returned to Jerusalem with great joy.*

–Luke 24:51–52

The Ascension: The absence of someone dear to us always makes us sad, especially when the absence is permanent, as is the case here. The risen Savior would not be appearing to the apostles again, nor would he be back to talk with them. Yet they shed no tears; on the contrary they went to Jerusalem full of joy.

Let us begin by considering the first aspect of this feast: the entry of Jesus into heaven, a cause for boundless joy. The Son of God, who loved us so much and endured such suffering and humiliation for us, was indeed worthy to recover his glory. Notice that his departure took place on the Mount of Olives, near the garden where the three apostles saw him prostrate with grief before the implacable silence of the Father, so gravely offended by sinners. Now God replies to his Son by granting him, so to speak, a resounding vengeance.

The Christ whom we see entering heaven is not the uncreated Word—in that sense he never left heaven (Jn 3:13)—but the incarnate Word with his human nature. There is something else too. Christ has not only introduced, in his own person, a son of our race into heaven. He has brought with him all redeemed humanity. Just as of old, victorious generals, granted the honors of triumph, used to lead a long procession of prisoners behind their chariots, so Jesus, entering his Father's kingdom, leads a multitude whom he has rescued from Satan's slavery and who have surrendered willingly to the Conqueror. We are Christ's prisoners, we belong to him, and with him we enter the dwelling place of his glory.

So it is an accomplished fact; we have entered heaven with Jesus and in him. Heaven has already been won for us. Jesus won it for us, and our sole concern is never to lose it; and here again Jesus comes to our aid. Not content with having prepared a place for us, he defends it so that it cannot be taken from us. Yet the efforts that he is making on our behalf do not end there. When Jesus withdrew from the disciples' sight on the Mount of Olives, two men in white appeared to them while they remained rooted to the spot and asked why they were looking up to heaven. Certainly, we should wonder at the triumph of Jesus, and think about the place which he has gone to prepare for us—our hope always being modified by fear. But our minds need to be fixed not only on the past and on the future; we ought to be occupying heaven *now*.

Before possessing in heaven the clear vision of the Divine Majesty, we can live there now by faith, which is something quite different from merely thinking about the joys of the hereafter. We can truly dwell in heaven in our minds. The Church does not deceive us with words. She makes us ask for

what she wants us to have: the mentality of an inhabitant of
heaven. We shall dwell in heaven insofar as our lives resemble
those of the angels and the saints. We shall dwell there whenever we conscientiously unite our prayers to the praise which
is eternally being offered to the Holy Trinity. For is not prayer
the soul's ascension to God?   is it?

# CHRIST'S WITNESSES ON EARTH

*"[Y]ou shall be my witnesses in Jerusalem and in all*
*Judea and Samaria and to the end of the earth."*

−Acts 1:8

The Ascension: Our Lord's ascension into heaven did not deprive the world of his salutary influence. He rose beyond the skies in order to fill the universe, and it is he who has raised up apostles, prophets, evangelists, pastors, and doctors of his Church. So Christ's body will be built up until the Church has formed a perfect humanity, fit to dwell with Christ in heaven.

The birth of the Church will take place on Pentecost. Today, Our Lord tells us that this will be the work, as was his own birth, of the Holy Spirit. It is not likely that the apostles would have gone back to Jerusalem from Galilee on their own initiative, yet we do find them back in the holy city. After sharing a meal with them, our Lord brought them along the road which led toward Bethany. Then he enjoined them to stay in Jerusalem until they had been endowed with strength from on high. This led them to ask him if he would immediately be establishing the kingdom of heaven.

The apostles once again fell back on their hopes of an earthly messiah. Yet they were not entirely to blame, for we can guess their line of reasoning: "Is that an impossible thing for one who has arisen from the dead? What could stop him from restoring the ancient kingdom?" Our Lord does not rebuke his impetuous questioners. They were thinking in terms of a restoration, and Jesus is calling them to a creation. They would willingly have rebuilt ruins, but instead they are required to build a new world. They thought to reestablish the kingdom of Israel, but the kingdom to be founded by them will ignore frontiers and embrace all nations. They were reckoning on solid political structures, but they would have to adapt the gospel to every regime and every human institution.

It is not now that the world will suddenly be changed into the kingdom of God, nor is it God alone who will cause that transformation. It is they, his witnesses, who will gradually modify the people's way of thinking. God will not strike his enemies dumb, but the Spirit will dictate words to the apostles which will have the power to convince. God will not hurl thunderbolts upon pagan temples, but the faith and charity of Christians will cause the idols to be forsaken and the temples to close one after another. Everything would happen as Jesus promised them, but nothing would come about in the way the eleven expected. Far from converting Jerusalem, they will in fact be driven out of it for a while, an apparent defeat that will compel them to preach the gospel outside the frontiers of Judaea.

As the Lord finished, they looked up; he was raised up and a cloud received him. The apostles did not mistake the reality of that cloud which had occupied such an important place in the religious history of the Chosen People; it was the sign of the presence of God. It seems that when the first moment of astonishment had passed, the apostles' amazement gave way to demonstrations of enthusiastic joyfulness. Now they were indeed in a hurry to receive the Holy Spirit so that they could begin to preach the gospel to the four corners of the earth. How much time must yet elapse before the glorious return of Jesus? It is not our business to know. We only know that his triumph will be all the more resounding according to the numbers of the elect. But that will depend on those of us who at this moment form part of his Church; it depends on our apostolic activity, which must be an essentially religious activity.

The temptation will always be strong to want to "restore the kingdom of Israel," which means to seek outside support and bring temporal influences into play. Beware, for it is not certain that you would use such power exclusively in Christ's service, and even less certain that you could obtain it and still remain faithful to the gospel. The last and final words of our Savior before he was taken up into the cloud define the only true form of apostolate: "You will be my witnesses." The faithful witness tries to imitate Jesus in abandonment to the Father, and in the joyful devotion to the service of others to the complete effacement of self. Jesus expects this personal witness from us, the witness of his living presence within us. The witness of a life is the only thing that cannot be disputed.

# THE WONDERFUL EFFECT OF CHRISTIAN CHARITY

*"Above all hold unfailing your love for one another, since love covers a multitude of sins."*

−1 Peter 4:8

Sunday within the Octave of the Ascension: St. Peter's advice on the practice of charity is very appropriate for the days between the Ascension and Pentecost, during which time the disciples gathered in the Upper Room and persevered, united in prayer.

It appears we are confronted with an aphorism current in the primitive Church; we find it in the two epistles of Pope St. Clement and among several second-century writers. A Syriac book of the third century, the *didaskalia* of the apostles, even quotes it as having been said by Jesus himself. St. James too, ends his epistle (Jas 5:20) with "cover a multitude of sins."

Charity bids us veil our neighbor's sins under Noah's cloak. It may sometimes be our duty to draw attention to another's misconduct, but in all other cases we ought, as Christians, to refrain from scandal for the supremely important reason that, since all sin is an offense against God, the respect due to him forbids us to call attention to evil. If we do not talk about it, we lessen its power to scandalize others. If we personally are the victims of another's sins, charity obliges us to keep quiet about it and to forgive the sinner if he shows his remorse; if not, then we must simply forget, thus overcoming evil with good. Instead of pouring oil on the fire of those wrongs committed against us, we should on the contrary cover them with ashes so that they may be quickly forgotten. If we hide them away, God will remember our good will and will forgive us our own trespasses, as we have forgiven those who have trespassed against us.

Now consider: "[W]hoever brings back a sinner from the error of his way will save his soul from death and will cover a multitude of sins" (Jas 5:20). With St. James' words the perspective has changed. No longer is it a question of fulfilling a duty; it is a question of a promise made by God to the Christian who shows his neighbor the exquisite charity of drawing him away from his sins.

Any further doubts we may have are dispelled by the words of St. Peter already quoted at the start of this chapter. Let us study these words attentively. St. Peter did not write, "In order to prove to your brothers that you love them, hide, smother, and veil their faults." He does not indicate the way in which we are to show our brotherly love but draws our attention to a strong motive for being charitable: because in loving your brothers, you will cover a multitude of sins. With him, as with St. James, "cover" has the meaning of "blot out" rather than "hide."

Whose sins is God forgiving in the text under discussion, those of the one who loves or those of the one who is loved? The sins forgiven are unquestionably those of the charitable Christian, because he has loved his brother with ardent charity.

Every act of charity brings to the doer the same indulgence from God. When the Lord calls the roll of the elect on the day of judgment, who will be the "blessed of the Father," found worthy to possess the kingdom? Of one thing however we can be certain: No matter how numerous the faults they may have committed, these will be blotted out in the moment of judgment by their charitable deeds. So it is indeed true that love covers a multitude of sins.

Can there be a more encouraging thought for us poor sinners? The heaven which Jesus has won for us is really within our reach. It depends on us alone whether the Lord will blot out our sins. Let us henceforth acclaim his infinite goodness, which wipes out our debt when we try to imitate his love in our dealings with our fellow men.

Let us be forgiving, veiling our brother's sins, which in God's eyes may not even be sins. Let us seek out the good that they do, or at least try to discover their good intentions, instead of automatically doubting their integrity, when we do not know them sufficiently to be able to judge them. And let us be generous in giving ourselves, in sharing our money too, even though times may be hard, and indeed precisely because they are hard.

# Jesus's Perpetual Prayer for his Own

*"I do not pray that thou shouldst take them out of the world, but that thou shouldst keep them from the evil one."*

–John 17:15

Sunday within the Octave of the Ascension: Jesus was going to leave the disciples whom the Father had entrusted to him. What would become of them? As long as he was with them things were easy, for he guarded them against every danger, the greatest of which was their own weakness. His miracles dispelled their doubts, his words convinced them, his look was sufficient to give them confidence. He was there to correct their mistakes. Sometimes he rebuked them with severity, but he always strengthened their courage. All that was now over. If only Jesus would agree to take them with him now.

The peril is not in the world itself, where Jesus was leaving them, but in the sin with which they will be in constant contact—sin which could kill their sincerity and their courage, their love and their life. As long as they fear sin, they need have no fear of the world. The gift which he made us of his Body and Blood preserves our souls for the eternal life to come. Jesus has returned to heaven, but he has not left us orphans. Let us praise God for leaving us here below for as long as he wishes.

If we were taken out of the world, who would proclaim the message of salvation? It is true that the sinners whom we must convert could lead us astray; but let us give thanks to the Lord, for he has found the means of keeping us from evil.

The dangers to which we are exposed during our sojourn on earth lie in our connivance with sin, which warps the conscience and weakens character. Holy Communion protects us from this double evil by establishing a bond of thought and will between Christ and ourselves. Thinking in us, our Lord keeps our conscience upright, refining its sensitivity and cleansing it of all compromise with sin. Because our Lord unites our will with his, he strengthens our weaknesses, allays our fears, and increases our vitality a hundredfold. Our Communions mean that instead of our Christian faith becoming worldly through the influence of evil, the world becomes Christianized because the Eucharist is sustaining us in the integrity of our faith.

In short, we are praying for Jesus to prolong the effects of the sacrament in order that his promises may take effect in us. Let God do with us what he will! The Eucharistic Christian also immolates himself to God's will; he loses his life to find it again, transfigured in that of Christ Jesus. The ascended Lord does not abandon those whom God has entrusted to him; he cares for them all the time. By our dwelling in him, we shall be preserved from evil; by his dwelling in us, he will sanctify the world.

# THE COMPLETION OF THE EASTER VICTORY

*Lord, send out your spirit, and renew the face of the earth.*

—Psalm 104:30, Responsorial Psalm on Pentecost

P entecost: This feast occupies a unique place in the calendar. It forms, as it were, a hinge between the two parts of the liturgical year, one of which is devoted to the mystery of the Son of God made man, the other to the mystery of the Church in which Christ continues his work.

We have previously described how, after being merely the conclusion of the great fifty days of Easter, Pentecost became an independent feast, being granted an octave in the eighth century to recall the week of the white robes. Henceforth it came to be considered not so much the conclusion of the first term of the liturgical year but rather the commencement of the second.

We shall have to consider the lessons it provides from this second point of view: On the one hand there is the miraculous birth of the Church which the Holy Spirit has sealed from the beginning with its essential marks of universality, unity, and holiness; and on the other hand there is the action of the Holy Spirit in the soul of each individual Christian. For the purposes of this present study we shall consider Pentecost only from the first of these aspects, as the coronation of the Easter victory and as the completion of the mysteries of Christ the Redeemer.

*how?* That which is completed on the day of Pentecost is, in fact, the mission that the Son of God came to fulfill visibly among us. Pentecost is not only a reproduction of Christmas; it is a replica of it. In Bethlehem, in a stable, the Son of God became a member of the human race. God and man became united in the person of Jesus, and we have good reason to fall on our knees before such condescension, *descendit de caelis* (descending from heaven). In Jerusalem, in the Upper Room, an even more astounding wonder took place on Pentecost Sunday: the Incarnation received a perpetual tomorrow. It was to be prolonged in the Church; it was man's turn to enter the divine family. The Son of God became man in order to confer upon "all who received him, who believed in his name, he gave power to become children of God" (Jn 1:12). "For the Son of God became man so that we might become God."[6]

Today there is joy upon earth, just as at the Ascension there was rejoicing in heaven. Jesus Christ is king of heaven and earth. Now he reigns in heaven, whence he will come, at the end of time, to manifest his glory upon earth. Between these two triumphs, past and future, the Church, guided by the Holy Spirit, is acting for our Savior here below. The Savior is acting in his Church—that is the equivalent of saying in a *human* society. Human beings! We know what they are like; we know their greatness, but we also know their wretchedness.

That Christians should have become the new people of God is fair enough—the former people of God were not so wonderful that we should have qualms about succeeding them—but the new alliance is radically different from God's old alliance with

6   St. Athanasius, *De inc.* 54, 3: PG 25, 192B.

Israel. Through the new alliance, concluded in the blood of Christ, God communicates his life to us, entrusting us with his work and his honor. No doubt, his Spirit is active in the Church, but it is no less true that we are the receptacles of divine treasures—from the Word of Jesus even to his Flesh and Blood. In the Lord's name men will speak, will judge in his stead, will remit or retain sins, and their decisions will be ratified in heaven. God has voluntarily deprived himself of his rights; how amazing that is!

When Joan of Arc's judges were trying to ensnare her in their artful traps, she calmly replied to them: "And in my opinion it is all one, God and the Church; and one should make no difficulty about it."[7] It was her honest opinion, and it is the opinion too of every good Christian. It may be asked whether the Church, composed of human beings, does not sometimes run the risk of usurping God's place. But that would be reckoning without the presence of the Holy Spirit. When St. Joan was asked by her interrogators if she would submit herself to the authority of the pope, the cardinals, the archbishops, and the bishops, she replied in the affirmative, but to the Lord first.

Let us make two resolutions. First of all to become more conscious of our sense of dignity, for we are the adopted children of God. Without blinding ourselves to our shortcomings, our unfaithfulness, and all those shadows that oppress us (they seem shadows because of the light shining within us), let us recognize the gift of God's presence in our souls.

In the company of those born into a new life, we shall march forward, confidently and energetically, toward that

7  *Wise Women: Over Two Thousand Years of Spiritual Writing by Women*, ed. Susan Cahill (New York: W. W. Norton & Company, 1997), 86.

great day when the glorious manifestation of the sons of God will take place—the day when the Spirit will have renewed the face of the earth.